WHY NOBODY
WANTS TO BE AROUND
CHRISTIANS
ANYMORE

AND HOW 4 ACTS OF LOVE WILL
MAKE YOUR FAITH MAGNETIC

Loveland, CO

THOM & JOANI SCHULTZ

Group
Real. Bold. Love.

Group resources really work!

This Group resource incorporates our R.E.A.L. approach to ministry. It reinforces a growing friendship with Jesus, encourages long-term learning, and results in life transformation, because it's:

Relational—Learner-to-learner interaction enhances learning and builds Christian friendships.

Experiential—What learners experience through discussion and action sticks with them up to 9 times longer than what they simply hear or read.

Applicable—The aim of Christian education is to equip learners to be both hearers and doers of God's Word.

Learner-based—Learners understand and retain more when the learning process takes into consideration how they learn best.

Why Nobody Wants to Be Around Christians Anymore:
And How 4 Acts of Love Will Make Your Faith Magnetic

Copyright © 2014 Thom and Joani Schultz

group.com | **lifetreecafe.com**

Credits
Editors: Jeff White and Amy Nappa
Assistant Editor: Kelsey Perry
Production Assistant: Cris Alsum

Library of Congress Cataloging-in-Publication Data

Schultz, Thom.
    Why nobody wants to be around Christians anymore : and how 4 acts of love will make your faith magnetic / Thom and Joani Schultz. -- First American paperback.
        pages cm
    ISBN 978-1-4707-1653-0 (pbk. : alk. paper) 1. Christian life. 2. Friendship--Religious aspects--Christianity. 3. Interpersonal relations--Religious aspects--Christianity. 4. Love--Religious aspects--Christianity. 5. Hospitality--Religious aspects--Christianity. 6. Conversation--Religious aspects--Christianity. 7. Humility--Religious aspects--Christianity. 8. Expectation (Psychology)--Religious aspects--Christianity. I. Title.
    BV4501.3.S3863 2014
    248.4--dc23
                            2014024427

ISBN 978-1-4707-1653-0

10 9 8 7 6 5 4 3 2 1   23 22 21 20 19 18 17 16 15 14

Printed in the Unites States of America.

CONTENTS

Acknowledgements

God blesses us with amazing people who surround us every day.

We're so grateful for our families—especially our son, Matt, and his wife, Shawna, who bring us such joy.

To those friends and co-workers who've shaped us and shared life with us, thank you.

Thanks to Cris Alsum, our awesome assistant who serves as our "super glue."

We especially thank those who've shared stories and insights for this book:

Brian Abbott
Craig Cable
Deb Gilmour
Gene Glade
Art and Nancy Going
Sheila Halasz
Cindy Hansen
Mikal Keefer
Jeanne Leland
Nathan Matz
Jeanne Mayo
Candace McMahan
Patty Stroup
Ali Thompson
Sophia Winter

And many thanks to our awesome team at Group for their creativity and input into this book.

INTRODUCTION

That's a pretty loaded statement. The word "Christian" means many things to different people. Some of those connotations are very positive. But, unfortunately, for many the word is highly negative. Like it or not, recent studies and surveys tell us the majority of people view Christians as judgmental, condemning, hypocritical, and—in too many ways to count—unloving.

We can all wring our hands or make excuses or try to defend ourselves. Or we can change it.

We recently released a book that challenges churches to focus on loving God and each other over, well, everything else. It's called *Why Nobody Wants to Go to Church Anymore: And How 4 Acts of Love Will Make Your Church Irresistible*. As expected, it touched a nerve (actually, a *lot* of nerves), and we've been overwhelmed by the response. One of the most frequent comments goes something like this: "I didn't want to like this book. But now I'll never look at church the same way again." Whether people were inspired by it or troubled by it, the book tackled a topic that readers couldn't ignore.

But it didn't end with churches. Again and again we heard from readers who said they wanted the 4 ACTS OF LOVE for their family, workplace, and other relationships. They realized if those Jesus-based principles could revolutionize the church, surely those same principles could transform individual Christians too.

We wrote this book because people asked for it. They've heard and experienced first-hand the sad stories of unloving believers, and they ache for change. They realize Christians are no longer known for their love for one another. If the word "Christian" is a loaded word, "love" is even more so—to the nth degree. So we decided to dig even deeper into these four ultra-practical acts of love and how they will change you, your relationships, and your world. They really will.

Why should *we* write this book? Why *us?* It's pretty simple: We're just regular people whose lives are filled with relationships. And we have a fair amount of experience (translation: we're getting older!), which means we've had a *lot* of practice. The opportunities for us to live out the 4 ACTS OF LOVE have been nearly endless, and as you'll see, our real-life laboratory is pretty much like your everyday life. We're married and have a son named Matt and a daughter-in-law, Shawna (we prefer daughter-in-love, not daughter-in-law). We have lots of extended family. We're blessed with more friends than we can count. We travel a lot, giving us the chance to make new and often unlikely friends (and we'll share some of our travel stories in this book!). We serve in our local church. We lead a company with a culture that practices living out the 4 ACTS OF LOVE every day. And during the past few years we've been hosting a social/faith experiment called Lifetree Café, where the most diverse people on the planet come together for an hour of conversation and stories that feed their souls. We've watched these radical, practical, Jesus-based acts of love change lives again and again and again—including our own.

The 4 ACTS OF LOVE have made our imperfect lives wonderful and full of wonder. And our every step is guided by God's Word. One verse that stands out the most to us is Hebrews 10:24:

> "Let us **THINK OF WAYS TO MOTIVATE ONE ANOTHER TO ACTS OF LOVE** and good works." —Hebrews 10:24

There's one other thing we want you to know about us (and it almost goes without saying): We're not perfect. Not even close. But our love is grounded in our love for God. That security and assurance of God's love propels us to love others. We take 1 John 4:19 to heart:

> **WE LOVE EACH OTHER BECAUSE** he loved us first. — 1 John 4:19

We believe those words with all our hearts. We also believe what that verse implies—that we simply can't love *without* God.

And we believe this about you: You're special in God's eyes. Nobody is like you and nobody has the unique opportunities you have to change the relationships in your world. We believe you occupy a unique circle of personal connections that are God-orchestrated "for such a time as this."

The God of the Bible has always worked through people—imperfect, average people. It's not during that one hour every Sunday when you're sitting in a pew and facing forward in silence. Remember: We don't *go* to church. We *are* the church. (A thought that can be simultaneously thrilling and terrifying.) The greatest act of our faith—love—shows up not beneath the glow of stained glass but in the midst of the fluttering fluorescents of our daily lives, when our shadows intersect with those around us. Magnetic faith works in the mundane, everyday interactions we have with people we know. That may seem ordinary to us, but to God it's nothing short of extraordinary.

Speaking of extraordinary, the foundation of this book is based on Jesus—the world's all-time greatest, most influential expert on the topic of love. Real, lasting, uplifting love. He wants us—you and me—to share his love to the people around us. We're Jesus with skin on. His hands and feet and voice and ears.

So we ask you not to merely read this book, but use it as a field guide for your life. Don't study it—try it. Its suggestions for relationships are meant to be experienced and practiced, like piano or sports. Loving others is a skill that doesn't always come easily or naturally. It can sometimes (let's be honest, *usually*) be risky. But we've found it's always a risk worth taking.

Just take one idea at a time if all these suggestions feel overwhelming. Every step moves you forward.

You're not taking these steps alone. We're cheering you on. And, most importantly, God promises to be working inside you and through you.

Why read this book? If Christians are called to love God and love others, then let's do it the most effective way we know how. Together we can make Christians once again known for their practical, authentic, welcoming love, which is nothing short of God's greatest miracle.

1

WHY NOBODY WANTS TO BE AROUND CHRISTIANS ANYMORE

Jerry was **THE KIND OF GUY YOU COULDN'T HELP LIKING** when you met him.

He was smart, articulate, and nothing short of charming. He always had a story to tell, always had a thoughtful insight, always asked sharp questions that made you wonder. His smiles seemed to linger longer than everyone else's.

Jerry was also a free thinker—someone who vocally and candidly questioned Jesus and Christianity.

A couple years after we'd gotten to know him, Jerry made a statement to us that planted its roots deep into our souls:

"You're not like other Christians."

Those five words were loaded with delightful—and dreadful—implications. We could only smile back, speechless. What exactly do you say to something like that? Was it a good thing? A bad thing? One thing's certain: We're going to spend the rest of our lives unpacking the depth of that declaration.

We met Jerry a few years ago. He was a regular at Lifetree Cafe, one of the "conversation cafés" we host every week for the local community. It's an hour of stories and discussion that focuses on a different topic each week—topics rarely addressed in a church. Every get-together takes place in a comfortable coffee shop–style setting and includes Scripture and prayer.

It's a new kind of faith-centered social experiment we've been conducting in an effort to love people who would never set foot in a church. Anyone is invited, no matter what they believe or don't believe.

Jerry didn't believe.

Yet he kept coming back. He challenged us. He asked lots of questions. He wasn't often satisfied with our answers. But it was a place where he was always welcome and accepted, a place where he knew that the people around him cared about him and what he had to say, even if they disagreed with him. It was, without question, a place of belonging for Jerry. A place where he found true friends. And possibly the only place where he met Christians he didn't dislike.

Jerry seemed mildly open to God, but throughout his life he had dismissed the Christian faith because of the people—other Christians— he'd encountered. While the sparkle in his eye was genuine, the smile on his face belied a man who was uncomfortable around believers.

Even the small things revealed his unease around Christians. One time someone mentioned the Eucharist during one of the group discussions. Jerry leaned over and whispered to me (Thom), "What's that?"

I whispered back, "It's like Communion."

"What's that?" Jerry asked.

At that moment, I knew Jerry had no experience with the church or its basic traditions. Yet the conversation that followed was a rich give-and-take of what Communion is and, more importantly, who Jesus is. I got to share the Gospel with Jerry, centered on his questions and natural curiosity. It was a respectful, beautiful, two-way dialogue I felt God had orchestrated.

Jerry faithfully (no pun intended) attended our conversation café for the last couple years of his life. But would he ever come to believe in God and accept Christ's love? The answer speaks to the very core of this book you're now reading. (We'll share the rest of Jerry's story later.)

"Are **YOU** a Christian?"

It's a question that makes a surprising number of believers uncomfortable in today's world. We sing about being "not ashamed," but many of us can't help but cringe a little when confronted with that simple inquiry. It's not because we're embarrassed to be Christians, but because so many Christians give our beliefs a really bad rap. Like it or not, we're guilty by association.

Recent research makes a pretty clear case that Christians are no longer highly regarded. We're not known for our love for one another—or anyone else, for that matter. We're known more for what we're *against* than what we're *for*. And it's not the fault of some marginal-but-vocal group of media-hungry extremists. The finger of blame points in one direction: the majority of Christians.

In their book *UnChristian*, authors David Kinnaman and Gabe Lyons reveal startling research that shows 87 percent of Americans view Christians as judgmental. And a whopping 85 percent of Americans consider Christians to be hypocritical.[1]

Ask yourself: Do I enjoy being around judgmental, hypocritical people? We sure don't.

Christians say they look to the Bible to guide their attitudes and actions, but, unfortunately, most of them are picking the wrong biblical examples. A recent study conducted by The Barna Group (a Christian organization, by the way) revealed that just over half (51 percent) of "self-identified Christians in the U.S." have the same hypocritical and judgmental attitudes and actions portrayed by the Pharisees in the New Testament.[2] (The Pharisees were those nasty, self-righteous religious leaders with whom Jesus was regularly at odds.) In contrast, Barna found that only 14 percent of self-identified Christians—a mere 1 out of 7—live out the attitudes and actions associated with Jesus.[3]

Let that sink in for a moment. If you took a checklist of the Pharisees' values versus Jesus' values, more than half of today's Christians would fall squarely in the Pharisee camp. And only 1 in 7 Christians could be described as living according to Jesus' example.

We have a problem.

When we hear that nobody wants to be around Christians anymore, it stings. The sad reality is that we Christ-followers have a lousy reputation. And we have nobody to blame but ourselves. Not the media. Not Hollywood. Not some imagined persecutors of the church. Not all those misguided sinners out there. It's us.

It's Not the Media's Fault

If you think secular media is responsible for the negative view of believers, think again. Only 9 percent of young non-churchgoers ("outsiders"), ages 16 to 29, attribute their unfavorable image of Christians to the secular media. Instead, most point to their personal experiences and conversations with believers themselves. No fewer than 50 million adults (that's one-fifth of all outsiders) blame their negative personal opinions of Christianity on their painful encounters with Christians.[4]

Where **DO YOU** Stand?

Below is an excerpt from The Barna Group's research showing how the researchers determined whether Christians aligned more closely with Jesus or the Pharisees. Take a couple of minutes to honestly consider how you have lived out these attitudes and actions in your life during the past year.

"The 10 research statements used to examine Christ-likeness include the following:

Actions like Jesus:

- I listen to others to learn their story before telling them about my faith.

- In recent years, I have influenced multiple people to consider following Christ.

- I regularly choose to have meals with people with very different faith or morals from me.

- I try to discover the needs of non-Christians rather than waiting for them to come to me.

- I am personally spending time with nonbelievers to help them follow Jesus.

Attitudes like Jesus:

- I see God-given value in every person, regardless of their past or present condition.

- I believe God is for everyone.

- I see God working in people's lives, even when they are not following him.

- It is more important to help people know God is for them than to make sure they know they are sinners.

- I feel compassion for people who are not following God and doing immoral things.

The 10 statements used to assess self-righteousness (like the Pharisees), included the following research items:

Self-Righteous Actions:

- I tell others the most important thing in my life is following God's rules.
- I don't talk about my sins or struggles. That's between me and God.
- I try to avoid spending time with people who are openly gay or lesbian.
- I like to point out those who do not have the right theology or doctrine.
- I prefer to serve people who attend my church rather than those outside the church.

Self-Righteous Attitudes:

- I find it hard to be friends with people who seem to constantly do the wrong things.
- It's not my responsibility to help people who won't help themselves.
- I feel grateful to be a Christian when I see other people's failures and flaws.
- I believe we should stand against those who are opposed to Christian values.
- People who follow God's rules are better than those who do not."

ARE WE BETTER
Than "Them"?

You know what it feels like to be rejected. It hurts. Deeply. Condemnation and finger-pointing have never made anyone feel valued or appreciated.

You also know what it feels like to be loved. Maybe it was by your parents or a sibling or your spouse or your partner or your best friend. You've most certainly been loved completely and unconditionally by God. It's quite the opposite from feeling condemned.

13

The difference is easy to tell…if you ask yourself the right questions:

Do you find yourself disapproving of others from time to time? Have you ever condemned anyone for their behavior or beliefs? Do you value being right about doctrine? Have you rejected people because they can't seem to get past their sin? Have you ever considered yourself better than some people? Do you tend to care more about upholding the truth rather than helping the broken? Do you ever find yourself thinking that you are more deserving of God's love than those people who just keep struggling?

*Or…*when people talk about you with others, do they say something like, "She's the one who just loves people" or "He's that guy who's always there when people need him"?

What would you rather have people know for certain about you as a Christian? That you're a self-righteous judge? Or that you're a fountain of God's overflowing love?

Sadly, we Christians have gotten the reputation of judging and condemning instead of pointing people to Jesus. We gladly preach John 3:16. You know, the passage that sports enthusiasts plaster on their forehead and street preachers wear as a sandwich board. The verse says, "For God loved the world so much that he gave his one and only Son, so that everyone who believes in him will not perish but have eternal life."

Interestingly, we typically fail to add the following verse:

> "God sent his Son into the world **NOT TO JUDGE THE WORLD,** but to save the world through him."
>
> —John 3:17

Let's not perpetuate the myth that once you're a Christian you're somehow immune from flaws and that it's now your job to highlight everyone else's weaknesses and misdeeds. Let's stop pretending that we Christians are "above" the struggling single mom whose kid has a hard time paying attention in Sunday school, or the alcoholic father who's angry at God because his son died in a motorcycle accident, or the teenager who has a million doubts and questions and yet keeps coming back to youth group hoping for more than answers. People all around us are battling through life, and we all need God's love—and his immeasurable grace—in our lives.

There's *one* way God sends his love—his grace—to those people in need. *Through us.* Through Christ's body here on earth.

If Christians aren't spreading God's love, no one will.

> "Most of all, **LOVE EACH OTHER AS IF YOUR LIFE DEPENDED ON IT.** Love makes up for practically anything."
>
> —1 Peter 4:8 (The Message)

FOUR REASONS
People Don't Want to Be Around Christians

So why is it, really, that people keep their distance from faithful believers? What exactly has tarnished our good standing with the world? We've talked with thousands of people and collected their stories. All of their reasons for avoiding Christians fall into four main categories:

1. "You judge me." People say they don't feel valued by Christians. They feel criticized. Whether it's their appearance, their mistake-prone past, or an endless list of other differences, they've been told they're not welcome among certain groups of believers. A common reaction we get from Christians who hear this complaint goes something like this: "Well, those people *should* feel judged. They're not living their lives the way God wants them to." Sigh. These kinds of responses from Christians just serve to prove the point.

And the judgment isn't limited to those outside the church. Our friend Patty serves her church by ministering to the youth. We know Patty, and we know she has a genuine heart for loving teens. But when the leaders of her church saw what she wore and the kind of car she was driving, they weren't sure she was the right person for the job. You read that right. Patty's clothing choice and old beat-up car weren't good enough for the church. So they decided Patty wasn't fit to minister to their kids. (Sadly, we hear stories like this nearly every day.)

Christians have a judgmental reputation.

2. "You don't care about me." "You don't care what I think or feel. You don't listen. You just lecture me." All it takes for people to feel this way is to visit a typical church. Virtually nothing about the way people experience church makes them feel personally cared for. They have no voice. They're instructed to sit quietly and learn the rules. Oh, and clap along while we sing together.

People have real needs that can only be met by other, caring people. (Remember, God does his work *through us*.) They're struggling, they're lonely, they're hurting. Our friend Sophia told us about a time her friend's husband was in a car accident, and the situation had become very difficult for them. Someone at church asked the hurting family about the accident, and the woman said that her husband was really angry at God for letting all this happen. The other church member's response? "Oh, that is NOT GOOD!" Rather than show love and concern, this Christian chose not to empathize or show support. She chose judgment rather than love.

3. "You're a bunch of hypocrites." We preach a gospel of love and grace, but we don't reflect those values when we interact with people who are different. People perceive Christians as acting as though they have it all together and know better than everyone else, especially in church and other social settings. They view us as arrogant and believing we're always right (also known as self-righteousness).

This reason gets the biggest eye roll from Christians. "None of us is perfect, and we don't pretend to be!" they say. But this complaint isn't really just about incongruous behavior. What bothers people is that Christians act like they have all the answers. That they've arrived. That they're only interested in telling others what to do. It's the same complaint Jesus lodged against the Pharisees. This kind of superiority is the opposite of the kind of Christ-like humility we need to exhibit.

4. "You act like God doesn't matter." People look at Christians and can't help but think their God is irrelevant to their lives. Believe it or not, people want God. They just don't want your religion. They're not looking for the "deep" theological trivia that many Christians obsess over. What they really want is to be reassured that God is real. They want to see signs that a loving God is working around them and making a real difference in people's lives today. But instead they see Christians who are preoccupied with doctrinal minutiae, policing morality, and saying all the right biblical things.

Nonbelievers watch Christians work so hard at controlling everything in their lives, as if God isn't the one in control. They watch Christians become outraged over every little offense, as if God isn't big enough to take care of himself. It's almost as though Christians don't really believe God is real. If we really believe in God, why don't we live like it? Why don't we look for ways he's working in the world around us, rather than working so hard ourselves to "prove" God to people?

What People
REALLY NEED

People have legitimate reasons for not wanting to be around Christians. Rather than be discouraged about that, we can view it as an opportunity to change. (Change *ourselves*, not them!) We're going to take an in-depth look at those changes throughout the rest of this book.

There's a tremendous opportunity we have to reconnect with people and make our love for them real and practical. We can begin by understanding their needs. How are we as Christians helping others where they need it the most?

Thankfully, researchers George Gallup Jr. and Michael Lindsay have uncovered exactly what people need. They've identified six basic needs of every person:

1. The need to believe life is meaningful and has a purpose.
2. The need for a sense of community and deeper relationships.
3. The need to be listened to and to be heard.
4. The need to feel one is growing in faith.
5. The need to be appreciated and respected.
6. The need for practical help in developing a mature faith.[6]

The good news? We know exactly what people need! And God wants to work through us to meet those needs.

"Dear friends, **SINCE GOD LOVED US THAT MUCH, WE SURELY OUGHT TO LOVE EACH OTHER.** No one has ever seen God. But if we love each other, God lives in us, and **HIS LOVE IS BROUGHT TO FULL EXPRESSION IN US.**"

—1 John 4:11-12

The **HARD TRUTH**

This may be hard to swallow, but it's true: We represent Jesus whether we mean to or not. People are watching us. And they don't like what they see. Most people—85 percent or more—say we're judgmental, pushy, too political, arrogant, closed-minded, and hypocritical.[7] And most of this comes from how they experience us in person (or, nowadays, on Facebook and Twitter). But even a cursory read of the New Testament shows that's not the attitude Jesus portrayed. The majority view Christians—and, therefore, Jesus—as quick to chastise instead of being quick to listen. So people see us—and our Lord—as condemning, not compassionate. We're perceived as those who circle our wagons rather than those who circle our arms around the hurt and broken.

We're meant to be Jesus with skin on. We're called to be the hands and feet of Jesus, showing his love to those around us. But very few Christians do that.

Our reputation needs much more than a makeover or PR campaign. It needs a thorough infusion of real, one-on-one, practical, authentic love.

To follow Jesus is to follow Jesus' example. To follow his example is to love others. Seriously, it's that simple.

A Story of **CHANGE**

Our friend Ali admitted to us that she used to be one of those "judgmental Christians." It surprised us to hear that, because we know Ali to be a loving and accepting person. She told us that, unfortunately, she wasn't always that way.

"I'm a recovering judgmental Christian," Ali said. "In middle school and high school, people knew me as 'Bible girl' because I kept a Bible in my locker and hung verses there. And that would've been fine…if it weren't accompanied by my holier-than-thou attitude. When people swore in front of me, without fail I would point my finger right in their face and say, 'Language!' Sometimes I would even quote Ephesians 4:29 to them. The message I sent during those years was this: 'Clean up your act. Jesus will never love you if you live like *that*.'

"As I got older, I learned to look at the plank in my own eye and let God use my lifestyle—not my judgmental words—as a testimony to others. I realized that Jesus lived a life of love, and he never made comments about someone's lifestyle until he'd built a loving relationship with them. He hung out with the scum of society and did so in a loving way.

"I wish I could go back and apologize to my former classmates. I'd love to get a do-over and show them love, not condemnation."

Amen, Ali.

Thankfully, it's absolutely possible for Christians to change our ways. (Or, to be more accurate, allow God and his gracious power to transform our lives.)

When others hold up a full-length mirror in front of us, we don't like what we see. We don't like that we've been stripped—just like the fabled emperor who has no clothes. We certainly don't like that we've been strapped with such a poor reputation. But if we're honest, we have to admit that "regular" people may have a point.

What if we, followers of Jesus, acknowledged that we have to make some changes? It's a lot like standing on the scale and realizing that a healthy diet and exercise are our only hope. If we're open to a radical transformation and to be all that God wants us to be, will others start seeing us for who we really want to be—another regular person created in the image of God and loved by God?

We have to face up to the fact that the emperor has no clothes. We want to blame anything else—other Christians, the media, Hollywood, those wicked sinners—as ruining our reputation, misrepresenting us as closed-minded, angry, and hypocritical. But our reputation has been built on the foundation of real people's real experiences with Christians. In the book *UnChristian*, the researchers noted that most people have had personal experience with believers. Nine out of ten people say they know Christians personally.[8] They're basing their opinions not on outside influences, but on the actual Christians they've encountered—people who profess to follow Jesus.

In a sense, that feels hopeless.

But we believe there's good news. There's no mistaking that we all—every one of us—hold the responsibility in our perception as followers of Jesus. In our very personal, one-on-one relationships with the people we encounter every day, *we* can make a difference. Together, we can change the world's perception. We're not at the mercy of the media or some evil external force. If we believe God's Word, we already have won the victory. We have nothing to fear. We can change others' perceptions.

There's hope!

19

LOVE Is Where We Start

For every follower of Christ, *love* is the beginning and the end of our faith. It should take precedence over everything we do.

Most Christians we've met claim to be driven by God's Word in how they live out their faith. Unfortunately, a fair number focus on minor issues in the Bible. These kinds of subjects—like alcohol, homosexuality, or baptism style—get minimum attention in Scripture and are usually not even mentioned by Jesus himself. Yet they all too frequently take precedence over the Bible's main message: that God loves us and wants us to love others.

That's the light we want to shine onto our path. If there's a guiding biblical theme that weaves everything in this book together, it's the idea that we love God and love others.

" I have loved you even as the Father has loved me. Remain in my love. When you obey my commandments, you remain in my love, just as I obey my Father's commandments and remain in his love. I have told you these things so that you will be filled with my joy. Yes, your joy will overflow! This is my commandment: Love each other in the same way I have loved you. There is no greater love than to lay down one's life for one's friends. You are my friends if you do what I command. I no longer call you slaves, because a master doesn't confide in his slaves. Now you are my friends, since I have told you everything the Father told me. You didn't choose me. I chose you. I appointed you to go and produce lasting fruit, so that the Father will give you whatever you ask for, using my name. **This is my command: Love each other.** "

—John 15:9-17

" One of the teachers of religious law was standing there listening to the debate. He realized that Jesus had answered well, so he asked, 'Of all the commandments, which is the most important?'

"Jesus replied, 'The most important commandment is this: "Listen, O Israel! The Lord our God is the one and only Lord. And you must love the Lord your God with all your heart, all your soul, all your mind, and all your strength." The second is equally important: "Love your neighbor as yourself." **No other commandment is greater than these.**' "

—Mark 12:28-31

" If I could speak all the languages of earth and of angels, but didn't love others, I would only be a noisy gong or a clanging cymbal. If I had the gift of prophecy, and if I understood all of God's secret plans and possessed all knowledge, and if I had such faith that I could move mountains, but didn't love others, I would be nothing. If I gave everything I have to the poor and even sacrificed my body, I could boast about it; but if I didn't love others, I would have gained nothing.

"Three things will last forever—faith, hope, and love—and **the greatest of these is love.** "

—1 Corinthians 13:1-3, 13

" We love each other because he loved us first. If someone says, 'I love God,' but hates a Christian brother or sister, that person is a liar; for if we don't love people we can see, how can we love God, whom we cannot see? And he has given us this command: **Those who love God must also love their Christian brothers and sisters.** "

—1 John 4:19-21

IMAGINE...

Imagine a world that views Christians as friends who are loving and accepting unconditionally. Who are willing to bring out the best in people through love. Who do what Jesus did. Imagine what it would be like if people experienced those who follow Jesus as "for" them, not "against" them. Always wanting the best for them.

Imagine if you could disagree with someone and still like and love them. We have many friends (even the two of us) who don't always agree. There's no shortage of things to disagree about. Politics, doctrine, science, education, the environment, money, raising kids, entertainment, etc., etc., etc. But we're committed to love, and that means it's possible to disagree and still remain in a healthy relationship.

Let's think about those six basic needs again and imagine:

1. **The need to believe life is meaningful and has a purpose.** Imagine God put you here to show—and glow—God's love to everyone around you.

2. **The need for a sense of community and deeper relationships.** Imagine God put you here to be the catalyst for bringing people together in relationship with others and him.
3. **The need to be listened to and to be heard.** Imagine God put you here to be the listening ears of Jesus.
4. **The need to feel one is growing in faith.** Imagine God put you here to help others grow in their faith while you're growing in yours.
5. **The need to be appreciated and respected.** Imagine God put you here to encourage and respect the people in your life.
6. **The need for practical help in developing a mature faith.** Imagine God put you here to walk alongside others as you mature in your faith while you also help others grow in a closer relationship with Jesus.

When we refer to "people" in this book, we mean anybody you're in relationship with. If you're married, it could be your spouse. If you're single, it could be your roommate. It could be your family, your kids, your parents, your co-workers, fellow students, or neighbors. Even the people in your church (who can sometimes be the hardest to love because we expect more from our Christian brothers and sisters).

What People **REALLY** Want

Make no mistake, people crave what Jesus offers. People may be leaving the church and pushing back other Christians, but they are hungering for God.

Consider these statistics:

- 91 percent say they believe in God.[9]
- 88 percent say faith is important.[10]
- 64 percent are open to pursuing their faith in an environment different from a typical church.[11]

People truly want God. They want to grow spiritually. They want a faith that matters in their everyday lives. Yet they stand on the sidelines watching us live as though God doesn't really make a difference.

We each can change that.

Let's go back to those four main reasons people don't want to be around Christians. How can we respond in love to each of those legitimate complaints?

We have some suggestions:

1. **You judge me.** People don't feel valued; they feel criticized. They don't feel welcomed by Christians. They're pushed away.

   * What if people in our lives knew that we accepted and loved them unconditionally? They're welcome just as they are. We call this RADICAL HOSPITALITY.

2. **You don't care about me.** People say Christians don't care how they think or feel. Christians don't listen and just want to lecture them.

   * What if people in our lives could count on us to listen and be willing to talk openly about the things they care about? Their thoughts are welcome; their doubts are welcome. We call this FEARLESS CONVERSATION.

3. **You're arrogant and hypocritical.** People hear from Christians that they know *the* truth and are right about everything.

   * What if we let down our defenses and admitted that we don't know everything, we don't have all the answers, and we all have something to learn? We're all in this together. We call this GENUINE HUMILITY.

4. **You live as though God doesn't matter.** People watch Christians try to control their lives through rules and doctrine.

   * What if we trusted the Holy Spirit to work and looked for signs of God's hands in our everyday lives? God is here, ready to connect with us in a fresh way. We call this DIVINE ANTICIPATION.

RADICAL HOSPITALITY. FEARLESS CONVERSATION. GENUINE HUMILITY. DIVINE ANTICIPATION. We call these things the 4 ACTS OF LOVE. Four practical, authentic ways of showing people that Christians really do love them. Four simple acts that, if lived out by believers, would completely change the way the world views Christians. Four kinds of love that Jesus himself modeled time and time again.

That's the kind of love the rest of this book is about. Are you ready to change the world?

Endnotes

1. David Kinnaman and Gabe Lyons, *UnChristian* (Grand Rapids, MI: Baker Books, 2007), 27.

2. The Barna Group, "Christians: More Like Jesus or Pharisees?" April 30, 2013, https://www.barna.org/barna-update/faith-spirituality/611-christians-more-like-jesus-or-pharisees.

3. Ibid.

4. David Kinnaman and Gabe Lyons, *UnChristian* (Grand Rapids, MI: Baker Books, 2007), 31-32.

5. The Barna Group, "Christians: More Like Jesus or Pharisees?" April 30, 2013, https://www.barna.org/barna-update/faith-spirituality/611-christians-more-like-jesus-or-pharisees.

6. George Gallup and Michael Lindsay, *The Gallup Guide: Reality Check for 21st Century Churches* (Loveland, CO: Group Publishing, 2002), 12-14.

7. David Kinnaman and Gabe Lyons, *UnChristian* (Grand Rapids, MI: Baker Books, 2007), 29-30.

8. Ibid., 31.

9. Pew Research Center, "'Nones' on the Rise," The Pew Forum on Religion and Public Life, October 9, 2012, 48.

10. The Barna Group, "Americans Are Exploring New Ways of Experiencing God," June 8, 2009, http://www.barna.org/barna-update/article/12-faithspirituality/270-americans-are-exploring-new-ways-of-experiencing-god.html.

11. Ibid.

2

If there's only one truth you take away from this book, we hope it's this:
FAITH IS A RELATIONSHIP.

It's not a subject to be studied. Not a point to be made. Not an argument to be won. It's not something you do on Sundays or how well you follow certain rules. And it's not an island—something you can compartmentalize from the rest of your life.

Faith is your relationship with God. In other words, to have faith in God is to have a relationship with God…and, by extension of God's love, a relationship with others. How you live out your faith is directly related to how you love God and the people around you.

It's All **ABOUT LOVE**

When the Pharisees tried to trick Jesus with a question about the most important commandment, Jesus responded with the most profound answer in all of history. "Love," he said. Love God, and love others. It's worth highlighting that both are *equally* important, according to Jesus.

That may sound like an easy answer, but it's not the easy thing to do. Following a narrow set of rules is far less demanding and far less wearisome—on those who follow the rules as well as those who make them. Tell me to do X, Y, and Z and we all know what the expectations are. But tell me to love and you've just made my life harder. When you love you have to forgive, sacrifice, endure, and be uncomfortable on a regular basis. Jesus never said loving others was the easy thing to do, but it is undoubtedly the right thing to do.

And it's so worth it! We all prefer to be around those who love us. We long to be in the presence of those who accept us and all our warts, who care for us despite our incorrigible resistance, who forgive us in light of our repeated offenses. Every one of us wants and needs and craves love, yet returning that love can be a constant challenge.

We believe that humans can't fully love others without the help of God. We talked about that with our friend Gene Glade, who expressed the thought beautifully when we spoke with him.

"How we see ourselves totally influences our lives," Gene told us. "It influences how we relate to others, what we get involved in, who we have as friends, whether we're shy or outgoing, how we dress. The list is endless, and it includes our relationship with God."

Gene said the greatest and truest view of how we see ourselves actually comes from God's view of us. Unfortunately, we let other factors influence how we see ourselves as worthy or unworthy of love. Perhaps it's how we think we're perceived by our parents, or how we think our friends and co-workers feel about us, or our abilities or lack of abilities, or our looks. The number of influences is different for each one of us.

But here's the real kicker. If we hold a distorted view of God, it translates into a distorted view of ourselves. If we see God as an angry bully who is mad at us all the time, that influences how we see ourselves treating others in relationships. Likewise, if we see God as critical and distant, we tend to see people that way. The 4 ACTS OF LOVE take a biblical, Jesus-style approach to God, love, and how we should relate to others.

How People View God

Approximately 90 percent of Americans say they believe in God. But not all those people picture God the same way.

31 percent view God as a dictator (angry, bossy, scary).

24 percent view God as a loving parent (kind, loving, forgiving).

24 percent view God as a distant bystander (a cosmic force that's left the world spinning on its own).

16 percent view God as critical (disapproving, unwilling to intervene).[1]

We also talked with Paul Young, author of the best-selling book *The Shack*, about how our perceptions of God shape our views of love. During his early childhood, Paul was raised in the mission field in Dutch New Guinea. By his own admission, his parents were preoccupied with ministering to the tribal people. Paul spent most of his time with the tribal people, who sexually abused him. As you might expect, Paul grew up with some dark and painful "crap" (as he calls it) in the shack of his own life. His view of God was twisted and misguided. Following some major mistakes in his adult life and close to committing suicide, Paul finally came to terms with how God viewed him. Amid all the ugliness and suffering, God came rushing in to Paul's shack, his arms open wide.

"But I thought you hated me," Paul said to God.

"No. It was you who hated you," Paul felt God saying.

We love the way Paul encapsulates the love of God: "I believe God pursues us with relentless affection, whether we know it or not, whether we want it or not. That's what love would do. Love knows we're lost, love knows we're broken, love knows we're blind. So love will pursue us, because that's what love does."

The **GOOD NEWS**

More wisdom from our friend Gene: "How God sees us is the only way we come to have the true view of ourselves. It is natural for us to see God as someone who is checking us out, when actually the opposite is true. His sole concern is for our good. And he stops at nothing to make that happen. God is the only one who knows the truth about you, and he alone is able to bring you to see that truth."

The Bible tells the whole God-story. It points us to the perfect love of Jesus. It is Jesus who helps us fully see God, God's love, and that God knows best. When we're secure in seeing ourselves loved (by God, for certain),

27

we can love ourselves…and then love others. You really can't love others when you don't love yourself. That's a truth that took nearly a lifetime for Paul Young to discover.

Colossians 1:15 tells us that "Christ is the visible image of the invisible God." Jesus was God with skin on. And now *we*, through God's Spirit, continue Jesus' legacy of being God's love with skin on. When we give love to others, we'll receive it as well.

Jesus showed us what loving others looks like on this earth. The 4 ACTS OF LOVE are simply a doable way to begin to love others like Jesus did. They're not exhaustive—the number of ways we can love others is infinite—but they are a way for us to live a life of love that will transform our relationships and put hands and feet to our faith.

And here's our promise: They're guaranteed to work.

> The importance of relationships for happiness is something that ancient philosophers talked about and contemporary science is proving it's true. That happiness is very much tied to relationships. For instance, when you look at people that are very happy, one of the traits that you see is that they tend to have a lot of very close relationships. Research shows that to be happy, we need to have intimate, enduring relationships, we need to be able to confide, we need to feel like we belong, and we need to get support; and just as important for happiness is we need to be able to give support.
>
> —Gretchen Rueben, author of *The Happiness Project*

It's essential that you know the truth about you and your relationship with God.

Our friend Gene Glade shared many of the ideas in the following pages.

Instead of being controlled by skewed perceptions (both ours and others'), let's take a look at the one person—the only person—whose view really matters most.

That's God.

And what does God think of you?

God is crazy in love with you.

God really does love you. He made you and believes in you. He's *for* you.

Our marriage is a great example of that kind of love. We *know* we love each other, we believe in each other, and we're *for* each other. So our marriage gives us a glimpse of what God's love is like. It's wonderful. It's fulfilling. It's life-giving. Yet as good as human relationships can be, they pale in comparison to the never-ending, unconditional love of God. Remember, God loves you.

The only true and perfect view of yourself must come from God's view of you.

Each of us needs to grasp the view that God, our Maker, has of us. Like loving parents totally committed to the well-being of their children, God has proven his love for us time and time again. He even sent his Son to die for us. We're that important. And he doesn't ever give up on us. Ultimately, God's view of you is the perfect view of you.

> "I have called you by name; **YOU ARE MINE.**" —Isaiah 43:1

Who you see in the mirror isn't the total picture. All those photos you post on Facebook and Instagram don't provide a perfect image of your being. That mistake you made yesterday in a fit of anger doesn't define everything about you. That talent you excel at better than everyone you know is really only a small part of your reality. Even your own lifetime of thoughts, actions, and experiences don't fully complete the truth about who you are.

But God—only God—knows exactly who you are. He views the entire you, the core of your whole being beyond time, soul, and body. He has more understanding about you than even you will ever know. And you know what he does then?

29

God relentlessly pursues you.

We mentioned that marriage gives us a glimpse of our loving relationship with God. The courtship before marriage illustrates part of that relationship too. We think Ryan and Amanda's story is a modern day parable of God's pursuit of us.

When Ryan and Amanda were dating, Ryan learned that Amanda had a secret dream: to be engaged and married on the same day. And he wanted to make her dream come true.

Ryan's investment in planning their destination engagement and wedding had risk written all over it. He invited nearly 100 family and friends to witness the engagement and stay for the wedding. They all had to fly to Miami. Remarkably, only one of the flights was cancelled—but it happened to be Amanda's. Even then, airline flights were the least of Ryan's worries.

How could he secretly arrange the venue? The catering? How on earth could he make sure her wedding dress fit? Could he pick the right colors and flowers? How could he possibly arrange the entire wedding service without her...as a surprise? It's not that he had checked out her plans on Pinterest. Ryan took an overwhelming risk in the hope that the love of his life would accept his proposal and fulfill her (and his) dreams. Would she even say yes when he proposed?

Ryan and Amanda make a great love story. But there's an even better love story...and you're in it. You're part of God's love story. God's done for you what Ryan did for Amanda. He knows your heart and your deepest desires. He's pursued you and expressed his extravagant love by sending Jesus for you. This much is clear: God wants a relationship with you.

God puts it all on the line for you. But he doesn't force himself upon us. Ultimately, it's our choice—just like it was Amanda's decision to say yes or no. And not unlike Ryan, God wants you to say yes to him and his love. That's because...

God wants you.

Have you ever stopped to think how valuable you are to God? How much you mean to him? We'll never forget a hand-scrawled photo frame with a picture of a little girl we were visiting in Thailand. Her family lived in a crude, shanty-like home a foot above the dirty water. Trash piles littered their home because her father made a living collecting garbage, sorting it, and reselling anything of value. There, above a heap of rubbish, hung a hand-colored frame encircling her picture. It simply said, "God wants you."

That little girl, living in a literal dump, knew what she meant to our all-powerful God.

God wants you too. In the center of all the endless throwaways, distractions, and debris of your life, God looks directly at you, his arms open wide and with a smile on his face, and says, "I want you."

But why?

God wants you...so he can do his most amazing work through you.

God thinks so much of you and me that he entrusts us with his greatest adventure.

Have you ever worked in a job where your boss trusted you to do his or her "thing"? Every day at our company, Group Publishing, we entrust our staff to "do 'our' thing." We put our confidence in them to carry out Group's mission. Each person is brought on the team to carry out a specific role to complete the mission. From dreaming up and vetting a concept to writing, editing, filming, designing, producing, staffing, managing, supplying, packaging, storing, financing, and sending. All the jobs include multiple gifts, and each person brings something special to the table that no one else can bring. That's because each person is uniquely gifted to best accomplish their part of the bigger picture and the greater good. We can tell you, as owners of a company, we value our team and believe they can do amazing things. (Otherwise we wouldn't have hired them in the first place.)

We think God works this way too.

Have you ever thought that God has chosen you specifically to do your part in accomplishing his mission?

We absolutely believe that. God has you placed in a specific time and place to accomplish his mission. Imagine God telling you, "You're hired!" Your job? It's actually pretty straightforward: loving others.

FOR SUCH A TIME
as This

There's a great story in the Bible about a beautiful young woman named Esther. Raised as an orphan by her uncle, she was placed in a time and place to rescue her people, the Jews. God used her unique circumstances to give her the opportunity to save the Jews from genocide. Though her situation was difficult and nearly perilous, her uncle cheered her on as he reminded her that maybe, just maybe, she was put there for a reason.

Sure enough, she was able to influence the king during this uncommon time and place. Esther took the risk, and God blessed her efforts to save thousands of lives.

We believe God still works like that today.

You don't need to be a queen or a king. God's not looking for heroes or champions. You just need to be open and willing for God to "do his thing" through you. Just think about this: *You* are the *only* person on the planet who has the unique relationships and interactions that you do. No one else spins in the circles that you spin. No one else has the personal contacts that you have. No one else.

No one but Esther could have saved the Jews from certain death under the Persian king. And no one but you can connect the people around you with the God who loves them.

This is the genius of God's big idea. He wants to show himself through us to others so he can reach everyone. From a human perspective, that's risky.

When Jesus ascended into heaven, we wonder if the angels had the following conversation with God:

Said the angels: "So, God, now that your Son, Jesus, is no longer on earth, what's the plan?"

God replied: "Well, one person will do what Jesus did and show love to another person. Then that person will show love to another person, and then that person will show love to another person, and then that person will show love to another person, and then...."

And on and on. That's God's plan. It's really that simple and really that amazing.

God believes in you that much? Yes. God has a purpose that he wants to do together with you. The Creator of the universe is counting on *you* (and the rest of us who believe in him) to be his partner. We're to "glow" Jesus' love in our own unique time and place to others. It's pure genius when you think about it. Each of us connects with others in our homes, workplaces, neighborhoods, schools, friendships, and churches. No one else has the same relationship influence that you have.

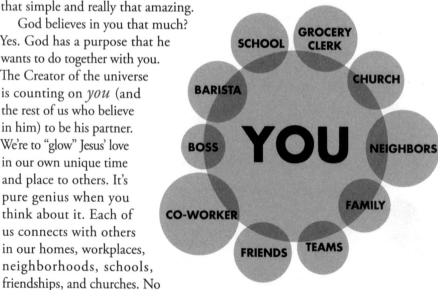

Nobody but *you* affects the people you do.

If you've ever wondered what God's purpose is for your life, that's it. Love the unique group of people in your life. Just. Love. Them. (We're going to spend the rest of this book exploring how to do that.)

Are you beginning to feel a tingle of excitement? A spark of exhilaration? Maybe even a twinge of fear?

Remember: Faith is a relationship, and God commands us, above everything else, to show love in our relationships.

Take a moment to wrap your head and heart around the incredible privilege and responsibility God has given you. God believes in you enough to trust you—with the inevitable successes and failures—to touch the lives of the people only you can.

Maybe that sends waves of anxiety or insecurity washing over you right now. Maybe the opportunity thrills you like nothing you've ever experienced before. Or perhaps you're somewhere in the middle. Either way, that's a lot of pressure.

"Me? God's ambassador of love to everyone I know? How can I ever be good enough for a challenge like that?"

But here's the beauty of this truth…

IT'S NOT ABOUT BEING GOOD. It's About Being God's.

That's how our friend Gene Glade puts it. We can fixate on our performance or our "good works." But that's entirely futile. Let's be honest: We'll never measure up. But that's the good news of the Gospel. Christ did it all *for* us.

We know as employers that our staff isn't perfect. We all make mistakes. In fact, we expect it. But that's not the point. We learn and grow from our mistakes. It's not about saying and doing all the right things all the time. With God's help, we can be exactly who God wants us to be. Just like all those examples in Hebrews 11, when we show God our faith he always responds. That's how relationships work.

We're not doing any of this by ourselves. We don't need to change or persuade anyone. That's God's job, and God's job alone. People don't like being around Christians anymore because they feel like Christians are always trying to fix them.

Let God do the fixing, while you love people through it.

Relax. When you stop focusing on yourself and your inadequacies, you're free to focus on others. If you're loving others, you're doing all God needs you to do.

Because of Our Total Dependence on God,
WE HAVE HOPE

Hopelessness can suck the life right out of you. Literally.

We once toured the Hỏa Lò Prison (also known as the "Hanoi Hilton"), that infamous dark, depressing prison in Vietnam where Senator John McCain was once held captive. We tried to imagine how utterly hopeless it must have been to be detained, beaten, starved, and chained there. What remains now are a few torture chambers designed to bring men to their breaking point. Even after all these years the dank atmosphere can give you the creeps. We can only imagine how much worse it was when filled with bloodied, despairing prisoners and merciless, menacing guards.

We had this in mind as we read about the "Stockdale Paradox." It's what Jim Collins in his book, *Good to Great*, describes as the difference between hope and hopelessness. He interviewed Admiral James Stockdale, a former prisoner of war in the Hỏa Lò Prison.

Collins asked Stockdale what made the difference between the surviving prisoners and those unable to endure that agonizing experience.

Stockdale said the difference was quite simple: The optimists were the ones who didn't make it out.

"The optimists. Oh, they were the ones who said, 'We're going to be out by Christmas.' And Christmas would come, and Christmas would go…And they died of a broken heart," Stockdale said.

The prisoners who survived were those who prepared themselves for the likelihood of a long and difficult captivity.

"This is a very important lesson," Stockdale said. "You must never confuse faith that you will prevail in the end—which you can never afford to lose—with the discipline to confront the most brutal facts of your current reality, whatever they might be."[2]

If anyone should be able to live with hopeful realism, we Christians can. "Because we have this hope, we are very bold" (2 Corinthians 3:12, GNT).

I (Joani) remember a conversation I had with a woman named Janet. She was bubbling over with excitement following a series of our conversation café get-togethers. She admitted that in the beginning she had felt scared and ill-equipped. She felt hopeless. But as her trust in God grew, she realized that God wasn't going to abandon her. Her relationships with those outside her Christian circle were blossoming. She confessed she wasn't that good at Bible history or explaining what God had done years ago. But she was great at sharing what God was doing in her life today. She sprinkled her conversations with natural ways she saw God in action every day around her. Janet's faith was becoming magnetic.

When we learn to depend on God, our hopelessness fades away.

You Don't Witness. YOU ARE A WITNESS.

We were recently in India and had the privilege of handing out warm sweaters and caps to children in the slums. Our team had to tramp through a maze of narrow streets littered with garbage and cow pies. As we made our way, Thom gripped my hand and steadied my steps. I (Joani) have multiple sclerosis, which makes it hard to walk and easy to stumble. Thom carefully helped me and found a nearby chair for me. All the while, Sheeba, our friendly guide, was speaking to the mass of children and their parents hovering in the background for the gift-giving celebration. Since we don't know Hindi, we smiled, dressed the children in the new sweaters, blessed them, and hugged them. What a simple, powerful act of love. Unbeknownst to us, however, Sheeba had used Thom as an object lesson. She pointed out Thom's kindness toward me to show Indian men how to treat their wives. In India, men don't treat their wives like that in public.

We didn't witness. We *were* a witness.

In Matthew 5, Jesus says to let your light shine. When we "glow" our faith, we let our light shine—naturally. There's no need to tell people when a light is shining. You don't walk into a dark room, flip the switch, and then announce to everyone that the light is on. They can see it for themselves.

Light is an amazing thing. Our eyes can see much farther than we think. Did you know that our eyes can see bright lights hundreds of miles away? In fact, on a dark night your eyes can detect a candle flame as far as 30 miles away.[3]

Don't witness. *Be* a witness. *Be* the light.

God Showed Us How to Live. HE SHOWS US JESUS.

First John 4:9 says, "God sent his only Son into the world so that we might live through him" *(The Message)*. What does it mean to "live through" someone?

Jesus is reliable and, once you get to know him, irresistible. His love never fails, and that's the kind of power source that never runs out. His is the kind of light that never dims.

Wouldn't it be great if it were obvious to anyone who knew us that we were living through Jesus? It can be.

We heard about a conversation between a churchgoer and a non-churchgoer. The churched person began describing Jesus to the curious woman who didn't know anything about Jesus. After learning about who

Jesus was, she said, "He sounds really great! If I go to your church will I meet anyone who's like Jesus?"

That's the big question. Will I meet anyone who's like Jesus?

Thankfully, we hear stories every day from people who encounter Jesus' love through those who "live through" Jesus. Jodie is a woman we met not long ago in a small town in the Midwest. She'd spent much of her adult life abusing drugs and disappointing most of the people in her life. Even when she was sober, she said she continued to make a lot of bad decisions in her life. Then she got to know Barb at the local conversation café. Barb "lived through Jesus" for Jodie. Jodie told us, "Never ever did Barb ever give up on me. She kept in touch with me and counseled me with making amends. Barb is such an amazing lady, and I am so proud to call her my friend (best one at that)."

Jodie saw Barb's light. Or, more accurately, saw God's light through Barb.

This is our hope and prayer for you. The following pages will bring you practical ways you can let Jesus' love live through your life. We call them the 4 ACTS OF LOVE. They're doable, they're realistic, and they work. They also take practice. Just like learning to ski or playing the piano or learning a new language, no one expects anyone to "get it" without trying again and again.

Like we've said before, you're not alone. We have the best personal coach in the universe! God, through the Holy Spirit, promises to guide us, encourage us, and pick us up when we fall. All along the way, in becoming more like Jesus, others will sense the magnetic pull of Jesus. Our own faith and actions will draw people closer to us and closer in their own relationship with God.

> **DON'T JUST PRETEND TO LOVE OTHERS. REALLY LOVE THEM.** Hate what is wrong. Hold tightly to what is good. Love each other with genuine affection, and **TAKE DELIGHT IN HONORING EACH OTHER.**
>
> —Romans 12:9-10

Let God Do **HIS JOB**

How do you know if the rest of this book is for you? Here are a few possible reasons for practicing the 4 ACTS OF LOVE in your life:

- Maybe you have a family member who's been hurt by the church and they're closed to any mention of Jesus.

- Maybe you have co-workers who taunt you because your Christian faith seems close-minded and they assume you think they're hell-bound.

- Maybe you belong to a group (sports, book club, political, work, you name it) and you're afraid if they know of your faith, you'd be ostracized.

- Maybe you know someone who shudders when looking at a church steeple—or when looking at you, because they know you're a Christian.

- Maybe you have gay friends who love God but feel rejected by the church.

- Maybe you have neighbors you really like, but they don't share your faith.

- Maybe you do have an agenda, but you need God to soften your heart.

- Maybe you know someone who was raised Mormon and is now a Buddhist who mocks the narrow-mindedness and judgmentalism of Christianity.

- Maybe you have a legalistic Christian friend who's quick to judge others (in spite of his drinking problem resulting in his third DUI.)

- Maybe you want to just be Jesus to people. But you don't know what that looks like.

- Maybe you're unclear where the line is between sharing how the Bible draws lines in the sand and how Jesus took the lines away.

- Maybe you wonder how to exemplify the love and grace that Jesus demonstrated when all that your friends and family see of Christians are the ones protesting at funerals, abusing children, and sleeping with the women in their congregation.

We could fill the rest of this book with the opportunities we have to "glow" the love of Jesus to those around us. To be honest, it seems daunting—even overwhelming—to imagine how we can pull off each of these mini-miracles (and not-so-mini-miracles).

Thankfully, there's good news!

To all those disagreeable attitudes, hardened hearts, broken relationships, and struggling beliefs, God says, *Hand them over to me.*

Matthew 11:28 tells us, "Then Jesus said, 'Come to me, all of you who are weary and carry heavy burdens, and I will give you rest.'"

God wants you to know we're in this together. God says, *You do your part; I'll do my part.*

But how does it all come together? You might be wondering, "What *is* my part?" We'll share more to help you in this journey—but a few things to keep in mind…

The Power of Experience

We have made some faulty assumptions in our efforts to share our faith with others. We assume that if we tell people what to believe, then that will result in them becoming believers.

But that's not how it works. *Ever.*

Our experiences form our beliefs, which then form our actions, followed by results.

For example, our family experiences shape our beliefs about family. Our school experiences shape our beliefs about school. If our experiences with church and other Christians are legalistic and punitive, those experiences shape our beliefs about God. And those beliefs shape our actions and how we interact with and perceive Christians.

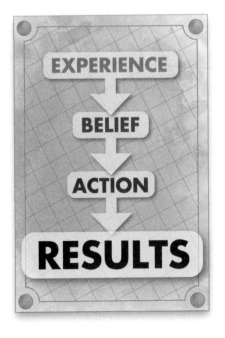

Love Takes Time— God's Time

Our world has gone into permanent overdrive—fast food, express coffee, high-speed Internet, instant messaging, on-demand TV, rapid rewards, the list goes on. We want our Google searches to be so fast that they predict what we want before we even type them in! We can hardly stand to wait in line, be put on hold, or pause an extra few seconds for large files to download. We want things *now!*

Of course, God can be faster than any of that stuff. Yet God's timing is nothing like ours.

Let God's timing do its work.

One Person Can Make a Difference

Never underestimate the power of one. The seed one person plants is all God needs to make a difference. Sometimes it makes all the difference. No matter where you are and who you come in contact with, trust that God will take the love you give and change a life in a way that's truly miraculous.

One of the greatest examples of the power of one touched us deeply when we interviewed Leon Leyson—the youngest Schindler's List survivor. Leon has since passed away, but we had the honor of an exclusive interview with this humble man. In his quiet yet powerful way, Leon recalled his life as a child in concentration camps and being saved from the horror of the Holocaust.

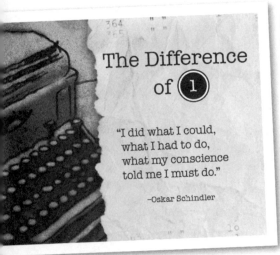

The Difference of ①

"I did what I could, what I had to do, what my conscience told me I must do."

-Oskar Schindler

Leon lost most his family, but he survived through the kindness of Oskar Schindler, who gathered hundreds of Jews to work in his factory. Schindler used his position, wealth, and power to risk what he could to save those he had the power to save. This one man saved generations upon generations of lives.

Whether you're making someone's day or literally saving someone's life, it's absolutely true that one person's act of love can make an incalculable difference.

People Will Experience God Through You

One more thing our friend Gene reminded us of is this: People don't decide on faith—they discover it. Their experiences with others is one of God's powerful ways for them to encounter God's love. Not by force or finger wagging. But by loving them with the love of Christ. By experiencing love through you, they are experiencing God's love.

You will become a God-magnet. Not only will people be drawn to you, but they will be drawn to God. And God's mission will be accomplished through you.

Endnotes

1. Paul Froese and Christopher Bader, "America's Four Gods," The Association of Religion Data Archives, http://thearda.com/whoisyourGod/fourgods/.

2. Jim Collins, *Good to Great: Why Some Companies Make the Leap…And Others Don't* (New York, NY: HarperCollins, 2001), 83-85.

3. Natalie Wolchover, "How Far Can the Human Eye See?" LiveScience, May 7, 2012, http://www.livescience.com/33895-human-eye.html.

3

THE 4 ACTS OF LOVE

2017 marks the 500th anniversary of the year a young **GERMAN MONK WROTE A REVOLUTIONARY LETTER.**

A letter that forever altered the course of Christianity. The monk despised, in particular, the church's practice of selling forgiveness to believers and using the money to pay for their church buildings, salaries, and other "ministry" expenses. He boldly challenged the professionalization of faith, claiming that Christians should have direct access to God and his Word.

His name was Martin Luther, and his letter, later known as *The Ninety-Five Theses*, ushered in a momentous shake-up we now call the Reformation. Luther's point? A relationship with God—as well as access to the Bible—should be firmly in the hands of the believers themselves and not left in charge of the professionals.

Over the last 500 years, Christianity seems to have returned to the kind of church that existed in the early 16th century. We now, again, pay professionals to do the work of faith. We sit in our pews and give money to others to do "real" ministry. Most of our tithes and offerings—upwards of 80 percent—go toward paying salaries and maintaining buildings. Many churches now employ large staffs of experts to teach, to sing, to minister to children and teens, to manage small groups, to coordinate outreach events, to counsel, to organize, to serve, to feed and clothe, and even to pray. We've unintentionally created a big machine in the hopes of reaching more and more people with the Gospel message. Instead, we've turned many people away.

Again, we Christians have gone astray.

It's time to reclaim the true intention for the church. It's time to unleash "regular" people in their everyday lives to be Jesus to each other. God intended for *all* of us to be empowered to embody love—not just the paid professionals.

This isn't an easy thing for us to say. After all, we (Thom and Joani) have built a thriving business over the past 40 years with the sole purpose of helping ministry professionals do their jobs as effectively as possible. Our company, Group Publishing, creates Sunday school curriculum, vacation Bible school programs, Bible studies, sermon books, training guides, and more, all in the name of bringing people closer to Christ. A worthy goal, to be sure. And it's been an amazing journey.

But a very different future lies ahead for the church.

No longer can we consider the church as a place we *attend*. No longer can we pour billions of dollars into buildings and salaries. No longer can we focus on attendance numbers as the measure of our success.

We don't *go* to church. We *are* the church. *We.* All of us Christians.

If a new kind of reformation is in store for Christianity, it's not to wait for the "professionals" to connect with God, but to return that responsibility to every one of us.

If that's going to happen, it's going to happen one way and one way only: through acts of love.

(A love, by the way, that's free.)

> "Let us continue to love one another, for love comes from God. **ANYONE WHO LOVES IS A CHILD OF GOD AND KNOWS GOD.**" —1 John 4:7

THE SOURCE of Love

Some people say you can love without God, but we don't think so. It's like having power without an outlet or a river without water. Love with God is real and powerful and life-changing. Love without God becomes self-serving, because we humans can't be our own self-sustaining power source.

You might call that sin. Sin is when *self* is the source. Self-sourced relationships break up; self-sourced people experience constant conflict; and self-sourced lives lead to abuse of food, sex, drugs, money, porn, fighting, greed, secrets, lies, hurt, emptiness, fleeting relationships. Too many marriages end with at least one person saying, "I'm leaving because I'm just not happy anymore."

Jesus shows us what it looks like when a person lets love flow from the Source—from God. People can *do* good, but ultimately it's about them *feeling* good. Our world is littered with broken shards of relationships. Without God, we try to fill our power source with temporal things that we think are love. But when reality catches up with us, we realize those things merely numb the pain so we don't feel the hurt quite so much.

It reminds us of the time we took a trip to the Gobi Desert. (Remember we told you we love to travel?) It's a part of Mongolia that's dry, desolate, and barren. The wall of the Himalayan mountain range literally blocks rain clouds from getting through. When we visited there a few years ago, we got the chance to witness something the locals called a miracle. As we were moving our stuff into our yurt (or "ger," as they're called over there), we heard a ruckus and ran outside to see what was happening. Our lodge was located along a riverbed, but it had been dry for years. Now a spring of water was drizzling from a rock formation encircling the lodge area. We watched as the thread of water began to form a narrow stream and then an ever-widening river. The children had never seen water in that spot before. To the villagers, it was nothing short of a miracle.

It reminded us of this passage of Scripture that predicted the coming

43

of Jesus: "Look, a righteous king is coming! And honest princes will rule under him. Each one will be like a shelter from the wind and a refuge from the storm, like streams of water in the desert and the shadow of a great rock in a parched land. Then everyone who has eyes will be able to see the truth, and everyone who has ears will be able to hear it" (Isaiah 32:1-3).

Water in the desert. In that little village in Mongolia we saw true joy and exuberance from people experiencing a life-giving marvel. It was real and tangible and made a remarkable difference in the lives of the people it touched.

That's what love does.

Love is something to be experienced. You don't study it, nitpick it, blame it, or just talk or sing about it. You do it. It's an action.

Love is not something that's left to the professionals. It's not hiring someone to build a pipe and then walk away.

Love dries up when it is not connected with the Source. Like trying to conjure water out of rocks in the desert, we're left high and dry without love.

Being plugged into the Source means being fully charged and engaged, being a vessel for that water to flow through. As Christians, we can't just *go* to church; we must *be* the church. Our world will change when we shift our mindset from thinking of our faith as a thing we do in a church building to the idea that the church is people. Paul Young, author of *The Shack*, told us, "You can't go to something that you already are."

Thriving Among the
DYING CHURCHES

While most church parking lots are left half-empty on a typical Sunday morning, one of the country's largest churches doesn't even have an official parking lot.

Chances are you've never heard of the "lead pastor" (actually, they don't like titles there), who oversees a gathering of more than 5,000 people every week in multiple locations in the area. This is no "multi-site" megachurch featuring a silver-tongued orator on a big screen. There's no professional praise band. No pipe organ. No fancy building. Nor is it a new church plant. It's been around for nearly 30 years. And unlike the majority of churches in America, it continues to grow.

Its leader is no 20-something hipster with a crown-of-thorns tattoo and urban haircut. She (yes, *she*) is 76-year-old Tillie Burgin, a white-haired, soft-spoken Texan whom the locals call Miss Tillie. She humbly leads Mission Arlington church in the sprawling low-income area between Dallas and Fort Worth.

Unlike so many other contemporary churches that tout the term "missional," this ministry consistently acts out real love every day of the year. Miss Tillie and her crew know what it means to be the church. They take their tagline seriously: "Taking church to the people." (It's true. We watched them in action!) The church family serves the local community daily with health care ministries, counseling services, spiritual support, and much more. Mission Arlington understands that "church" doesn't mean sitting in a Sunday service. "Church" is being the hands and feet of Jesus.

They simply show love to people who need it.

Looking in **THE MIRROR**

Have you ever woken up one day and realized there was something so fundamental, so basic, that you couldn't believe you missed it all these years?

Maybe that's what's happened to Christians today. When we take a hard look in that mirror, we must confess:

Christians *talk* love, but we don't really *do* love.

Even a newborn baby knows love. No matter the age, income, education, gender, ethnicity—humans know and need love. We were created out of love to love, to be in relationship with our God and each other. When we experience love, we experience God. We get a taste of the Divine, the Source of love. And that happens on earth as people become the channel for God's love to flow.

Let's look in the mirror again. Our churches talk love, but we've forgotten that what we do is more important than what we say. Actions always speak louder than words. Our friend Nathan says, "People today don't listen. They watch."

So let's look in the mirror, remembering that faith is a relationship.

If we want to help people pursue a relationship with God, why wouldn't that look like how people pursue a relationship? Think of any good, healthy relationship. How does that develop and grow?

We've been married for 30 years. Our bond is not an academic subject. Our relationship did not develop through a series of academic classes. Had

45

that been the case, our relationship would've been dead on arrival. Had one of us stood and lectured while the other passively listened, our love could never have grown. Had one of us handed out little worksheets to fill in while the other spoke, our dating life would have crashed on date number one.

Our relationship is not built on mastering loads of historical facts and bits of information about each other. In fact, to this day we still can't do a great job of keeping each other's relatives straight. Our love is not built on an academic historical exercise. It has developed and deepened through an ongoing series of shared experiences, rich and honest conversation, and working through the thick and thin of real life together.

We believe faith in God develops much like other relationships. That means it's rarely a strict linear process. It's like relationships with other humans—messy, nonsequential, filled with ups and downs, lots of forwards and backwards. Sure, a relationship includes knowledge and information, but that's not what makes a relationship tick. God can't be reduced to theological nitpicking and theoretical musings. God is real, alive, and active in our world and is ultimately relational.

So, faith is a relationship with the living God…
who is real…
who reveals himself in Jesus…
who, through the Holy Spirit, reveals himself in people today.
Faith comes to life through relationships—loving God and loving others.

ARE YOU a Loving, Jesus-Centered, Relationship-Oriented Christian?

Pause a moment for an honest look in the mirror. When others interact with you, would they say you are...

PATIENT?
Almost All the Time ⟵————————————————⟶ Rarely

KIND?
Almost All the Time ⟵————————————————⟶ Rarely

NOT JEALOUS?
Almost All the Time ⟵————————————————⟶ Rarely

NOT CONCERNED WITH COMPARISONS OR COMPETITION?
Almost All the Time ⟵————————————————⟶ Rarely

NOT PRIDEFUL?
Almost All the Time ⟵————————————————⟶ Rarely

NEVER RUDE TO THEM OR DEMANDING OF THEM?
Almost All the Time ⟵————————————————⟶ Rarely

NOT IRRITABLE?
Almost All the Time ⟵————————————————⟶ Rarely

NOT SOMEONE TO REMEMBER THE WRONG THINGS THEY'VE DONE?
Almost All the Time ⟵————————————————⟶ Rarely

NOT SOMEONE TO KEEP A GRUDGE AGAINST THEM OR OTHERS?
Almost All the Time ⟵————————————————⟶ Rarely

NOT SOMEONE WHO REJOICES AT THE INJUSTICES IN THEIR LIFE?
Almost All the Time ⟵————————————————⟶ Rarely

REJOICES WHEN TRUTH WINS OUT IN A GOOD WAY FOR THEM?
Almost All the Time ⟵————————————————⟶ Rarely

NEVER GIVES UP ON THEM?
Almost All the Time ⟵————————————————⟶ Rarely

NEVER LOSES FAITH IN THEM?
Almost All the Time ⟵————————————————⟶ Rarely

HOPEFUL?
Almost All the Time ⟵————————————————⟶ Rarely

The ONE THING

When it comes to finding clarity of purpose, we love Jesus' encounter with Mary and Martha. Jesus told the sisters that "only one thing" truly mattered. That "one thing" was exemplified in the relationship being nurtured between Jesus and Mary.

That's it. That's the one thing. The big deal. It's *relationship* that drove Jesus' ministry. And it's what he prepared his disciples to replicate.

Jesus showed that growing a relationship with him resembles how we grow a good relationship with other people. But he was criticized for that. The religious elite called him "a glutton and a drunkard, and a friend of tax collectors and other sinners" (Matthew 11:19).

But his mission was clear. It was all about the relationship—with him and with others. That mission dominated everything he did and said. Building the relationship was more important than tradition. More important than formality. More important than religious taboos, such as picking grain on the Sabbath.

It's that devotion to relationship that drives our passion to relate better with those who do not yet have an actual relationship with Jesus, as well as those who have left it behind.

So what does a Jesus-centered, relationship-oriented Christian love look and sound like? A very smart and talented guy named Paul said it best:

"If I could speak all the languages of earth and of angels, but didn't love others, I would only be a noisy gong or a clanging cymbal."

How many intelligent Christians—the armchair theologians, academicians, teachers, and preachers—can impress everyone they know with their in-depth knowledge of the intricacies of Scripture? If listeners walk away without experiencing love, they've done nothing but caused a commotion.

"If I had the gift of prophecy, and if I understood all of God's secret plans and possessed all knowledge..."

How often have we been lured by witty three-point sermons, clever four-letter acronyms, profound five-step strategies, or the endless parade of preaching-to-the-choir Christian books? If learners walk away without love, all our efforts in preaching and teaching are truly meaningless.

"And if I had such faith that I could move mountains, but I didn't love others, I would be nothing."

How many times have we tried to inspire people to greater faith by piling up the to-do lists and comparisons while pointing out all the

48

guilt, inadequacies, and shortcomings? If the hurting walk away without genuine, selfless love, every single thing we say and do will amount to a hill of rotting beans.

"If I gave everything I have to the poor and even sacrificed my body, I could boast about it; but if I didn't love others, I would have gained nothing" (1 Corinthians 13:1-3).

How often do we focus on social justice, wars on poverty, service projects, good deeds, sacrificial living that make us feel good about ourselves…and do it without a personal, real love for individuals? If the helpless walk away without love, we're getting nowhere.

On top of all of that, here's the most astonishing, freeing, scary thing: *"Love never gives up, never loses faith, is always hopeful, and endures through every circumstance"* (1 Corinthians 13:7).

What would happen if we really believed that?

We decided to take 1 Corinthians 13 to heart. Rather than pour all our energies into finding new and innovative ways to *teach people about God,* we wondered what it would look like if we focused on helping people *grow in a relationship with God.*

OUR BOLD (and Scary) EXPERIMENT

This is the story of how we "discovered" the 4 ACTS OF LOVE.

You know God is up to something when he wakes you up in the middle of the night. Isn't that what happens in the Bible? That's what happened to me (Thom).

Like a recurring dream, a radical concept unfolded. God helped us weave our years of serving the church into a unique concept for "such a time as this." Just like a reluctant Esther determined to save her people, we began to experiment with the concept we would eventually call Lifetree Café.

Here's what God had given us to work with:

- decades of experience as a company that knows and loves the church,
- what we already know about the transformative power of relational, experiential, applicable, and learner-based learning for all ages,
- mountains of research on church, generations, and culture,
- a love of adventure and risk,

49

- a desire to change the world,

- a talented team,

- a childlike faith believing the same power that raised Jesus from the dead is working in us,

- a passion to live out loving God and loving others, and

- an openness to fail.

So, like good "church people," we formed a committee. Well, not exactly. We challenged a small group of "Groupies" to meet at least once a week over breakfast, Bible study, and prayer for more than a year.

We ate scrambled eggs, yogurt, and granola. We guzzled cups of coffee and juice. And we grappled. We uncovered everything we could about the status quo of Christianity, the cultural trends, what creative thinkers thought, what was working, and what was not. We prayed for guidance and God's insights. We met to wrestle, question, and wonder.

After all that time grappling, we decided to bring others into our fledgling think tank. We invited a few guests—some "church-inclined" and some "church-declined"—all sharp thinkers who would tear apart our ideas. And that they did. We proposed a concept that we believed would reach the ever-growing, non-church-going population.

The good news? We discovered people outside the church aren't opposed to God.

They're just suspicious and tired of the way Christians have packaged their faith. We heard from those who rejected church. We respected their input. And we wanted to find a fresh way to make Jesus magnetic through our actions.

Finally, after meeting for well over a year, one exasperated team member stood up and exclaimed, "Let's just do it!"

We all jolted awake like dead batteries come to life. He was right. We'd become paralyzed just like the church we so desperately were trying to change. How'd that happen? How easy it is to wallow in information overload and fear. It was time to step out in faith and give birth to something new, bold, and not a little bit scary. We called it a conversation café, and we named it Lifetree Café.

Things didn't start out so well.

Like planting a seed, our hands got dirty. We made tons of mistakes. It was messy and slow. We prayed for patience and help. We took every opportunity to learn from our mistakes and prune our fledgling little idea. And there was no shortage of things to keep us humble.

Take our very first Lifetree Café event, for example.

We'd carefully plotted and planned an hour of experiences to foster conversation and relationships that would create an environment for God to show up. Well, he did, but not how we expected. Our theme, "Give thanks in all circumstances," would prove to be an all-too-needed inspiration.

It was a Sunday evening at 6:30. We met in the coffee shop in our company headquarters around small tables. One of our team members had enthusiastically invited a batch of skeptical pastor friends to check out this "new thing" we'd cooked up. We started with a couple of get-acquainted activities with the mixed ages of about 25 people.

We had planned a live interview with our friend, Craig DeMartino, an amazing survivor of a 100-foot mountain-climbing fall. He was a living miracle, and he had a remarkable story to tell. His interview began…and so did the building's alarm system. An ear-piercing blast filled the air. Everyone cringed. None of us could figure out how to shut off the alarm system that was just doing its job of alerting us of after-hours intruders. Craig and I (Thom) shouted above the din, trying to share how the right attitude gets us through. Then finally, someone disarmed the alarm. Ahhhh.

Then it was time for our creative prayer station experience where individuals would ponder and pray as they connected with God. And then…the blasted alarm went off *again!* After a few more unbearable minutes, we figured out how to shut it off.

The group left, gracious and kind. Most never returned. It was terrible.

We drove home, and I (Joani) was in tears. We'd planned so hard. Hours and hours of thought and preparation. Why would God allow our first big night to be such a disaster?

The next morning, God revealed something even bigger to us: *It's not about you. It's not about your perfectly planned performance. It's about ME. And I want you to give thanks in all circumstances. Remember?*

Okay. First lesson learned. Lifetree Café started out the hard way.

Then things started to get interesting.

As we experimented with this new way to "be the church," we gradually developed a mixture of elements that created a place where real relationships—with God and others—can grow every time people come. A place where all kinds of people, from longtime believers to nonbelievers and everyone in between, gather to hear inspiring stories and engage in conversation on a different topic every week. It's led entirely by volunteers and revolves around being a safe, welcoming environment where everybody gets to share their own thoughts and stories.

Lifetree Café became a very "non-churchy" place where people could connect with God. Now there are hundreds of Lifetree Cafés all over North

THE 4 ACTS OF LOVE

America, and more are added every week. Thousands of people gather each week in groups that number anywhere from 10 to 50. Nearly every day we hear amazing stories of people's lives being touched and transformed by God…through the Christ-like love of those they get to know during the Lifetree Café get-togethers.

Throughout this experience we've been blown away by the things God has shown us about how to love other people. It's through our bold (and scary) experiment of Lifetree Café and many other ministry endeavors that we've learned the power of what we now call the 4 ACTS OF LOVE.

What Happens at a Conversation Café?

Our conversation café was designed to connect with the roughly 80 percent of Americans who don't go to church. It's a different way to "be" the church—a way to build relationships with people who would never step foot inside a church. A way to show them God's love and meet their needs every time we connect.

One of the hallmarks of Lifetree Café is that we deal with a wide variety of everyday, practical subjects like happiness, health, and finances. But we also aren't afraid to tackle the toughest topics—guns, immigration, marijuana, homosexuality, politics, other beliefs—things you'd never expect to 1) be discussed fairly in a church, if at all, or 2) be discussed in a friendly, safe, and nonjudgmental atmosphere. People often ask us, "How do you prevent shouting matches and name calling? Don't people get mad and defensive? Do they ever throw tables at each other?"

▼

At Lifetree Café, people sit around tables, they don't throw them. We set ground rules of respect for others. We can disagree and still be friends.

And it works! For many years we've watched people listen respectfully to the opposing side of their point of view. They ask wondering questions such as, "What about the other person's opinion makes sense?" "Why might they think and feel that way?" and "What could I do to show I care for them?"

It's all about respect. We know that none of us is 100 percent right about everything, and we know that we're never all going to agree. But we also know that faith is a relationship, and at the end of the day love is the one thing that breaks through.

The 4 **ACTS OF LOVE**

With God as the source, we've found the 4 ACTS OF LOVE to be fully powerful, authentic, life-changing ways for Christians to share God's love with the unchurched, the dechurched, and the churched. The 4 ACTS OF LOVE are, in essence and in practice, *how* to grow faith as a relationship.

Before we dive deep into each of the 4 ACTS OF LOVE, let's do a quick overview of what they are and how they relate to the most common reasons people don't want to be around Christians anymore:

When people say...	Imagine Jesus saying...	Christians practice...
"I feel judged."	"You're welcome just as you are."	RADICAL HOSPITALITY
"I don't want to be lectured. You don't care what I think."	"Your thoughts are welcome; your doubts are welcome."	FEARLESS CONVERSATION
"Church people are a bunch of hypocrites."	"We're all in this together."	GENUINE HUMILITY
"Your God is irrelevant to my life."	"God is here, ready to connect with you in a fresh way."	DIVINE ANTICIPATION

53

These 4 ACTS OF LOVE—RADICAL HOSPITALITY, FEARLESS CONVERSATION, GENUINE HUMILITY, and DIVINE ANTICIPATION—will make your faith magnetic because *Jesus* is magnetic. They really work, and we can honestly tell you we've witnessed the water flow in this desert countless times, week after week, for the last few years. And the 4 ACTS OF LOVE are integrated into our everyday interactions and our everyday relationships.

The principles and practices that we've learned from doing Lifetree Café are doable for any Christian. Churches today may be training believers to share their faith, but it's like teaching swimming lessons without ever letting people get in the pool. Lifetree Café has been our swimming pool, and now the 4 ACTS OF LOVE can be yours.

Of course, you don't have to open a conversation café to put this kind of love into action. Here's what we know from our experience with thousands of people over the last three or four years: When the four cries (why nobody wants to be around Christians anymore) meet these four Jesus-centered values, God's Spirit can't help but gush forth in miraculous ways.

"Dear friends, **LET US CONTINUE TO LOVE ONE ANOTHER, FOR LOVE COMES FROM GOD.** Anyone who loves is a child of God and knows God. But **ANYONE WHO DOES NOT LOVE DOES NOT KNOW GOD,** for God is love."

—1 John 4:7-8

The Church That
WOULDN'T BURN

Samarai Island was a once-thriving village in the territory of Papua New Guinea. While on tour there, we walked past a decrepit, crumbling Anglican church. We learned that during World War II enemy forces burned the entire village with one exception: the church. Multiple times soldiers torched the building, but it would not burn. So it still stands today—although a sad, decaying ruin of its former self. The timbers are rotting and the roof is nearly gone. Yet the legend of it standing through the fire lives on. Is this a parable for Christians today? The church has miraculously avoided destruction in the past, yet today it appears to be falling apart.

God will not give up on his children. For centuries, in spite of our shortcomings, Jesus' followers continue on in their faith. Matthew 16:18 says, "Upon this rock I will build my church, and all the powers of hell will not conquer it." We don't believe Christians will disappear into oblivion. But we can't look in the mirror and walk away. Now is the time to take a deep breath and prepare to make some remarkable changes that will undoubtedly manifest some remarkable results.

We firmly believe that every Christian—including you—can use the 4 ACTS OF LOVE to make your faith magnetic.

TWO THINGS
to Keep in Mind

In the next few chapters we're going to show you some profound, practical, and effective ways to show God's love to others and make your faith magnetic. Before we jump headlong into the 4 ACTS OF LOVE, there are a couple of things we'd like to mention about how to approach those people with whom you share God's love.

First, **be in relationship**. If you want to share your faith, remember that faith is a relationship. It's not a subject to be discussed or a point that must be persuaded. The other person must know that you care about them as a person; indeed, you *must* care about them as a person. They'll sense immediately whether you care about the relationship or care about being right.

Our good friend Jeanne told us a story about a woman she ran into in a coffee shop. She hadn't seen the woman in about a year and had only met her briefly once at a Bible study. Jeanne remembered the woman being pregnant and asked how she was doing. To Jeanne's surprise, the young woman shared she had miscarried. Jeanne told her how sorry she was and later that week sent flowers to her house with a card that simply said, "Thinking of you. Jeanne." A couple weeks later the woman tracked Jeanne down and called her. She said her mother lived in another state, and she wondered if Jeanne would be willing to go on a walk with her just to talk.

"I remember the feeling of honor and privilege that she asked that of me," Jeanne said. "It also made me realize how important it is for us to spend time together with other women and moms and reflect Christ's love as they live their lives. I remind myself that God gave me two ears and one mouth for a reason."

Jeanne knew she couldn't truly touch this woman's life without building a relationship with her first. She did, and she made a lasting impact on that young woman's life.

Second, **get permission**. Don't force yourself or your ideas. God patiently waits for us to join him, and we can follow his example. No one wants to be a "project." No one wants to be another notch in your spiritual belt. If you love them and care about them as a person first, then they'll open up themselves to you and give you the blessing of going deeper into their lives.

Love doesn't have a secret agenda. We love going to film festivals, and we've seen our fair share of documentaries. It's so obvious when the filmmaker has an agenda. But at film festivals we often get the chance to hear directly from the filmmakers and get a deeper understanding of their point of view. It's refreshing when the directors and producers have to admit that the world we live in isn't exactly black and white. There's a lot of gray. The "bad guys" aren't usually as evil as they're portrayed, and the "good guys" are far from perfect themselves. Sadly, so much of the animosity happens when either side refuses to genuinely love the other and stop demonizing the person and their point of view.

That's why it's so important to love others unconditionally. Don't make people go through your checklist before you'll accept them. Be "for" them. Believe us, people can always tell when you truly care about who they are. They can see right through agenda-driven love.

Just love, and let God do God's job. You can't change or fix someone else. You can't go into a marriage hoping to fix or change your spouse. The same goes for any relationship. We can't change anyone. Only God can do that.

"THE LORD LOOKS at the heart."

—Romans 12:9-10

STANDING on the Edge

On a trip to Vanuatu (a group of islands in the Pacific), we found ourselves taking a journey into the unknown. Picture a dark, completely black night where you literally can't see your hand in front of your face. We rode inside a one-eyed pickup truck, lunging like a hungry bear over the rough road. The natives dropped us off near a stone-lined ashen trail. We followed two lanky teenage guides wrapped in blankets to ward off the blustering wind. We hiked up, up, up...and then KABOOM! A deafening sound followed by an orange glow that lit up the rocky terrain around us. We were shocked to find ourselves standing inches from the edge of a boiling volcanic crater! Never would we have agreed to walk this path if we'd known where they were taking us. But we would never trade the experience of what we witnessed: the might, majesty, and power of God's awesome creation. It was something very few get to experience. But there we were, toe to toe with one of the most powerful forces on the planet.

Willing to take the risk, we had followed our guides who'd been there many times before. And we lived to tell about it.

You're standing with us now on a similar edge. You may not be comfortable with the simmering cauldron beneath your feet. But if we're willing to face it—together and with God—we'll get to explore something truly life changing.

4 RADICAL HOSPITALITY

Sometimes you can't script **A BETTER STORY THAN REAL LIFE.**

The Lifetree Café topic for the week was "Temptation: Why Good Men Go Bad." The hour promised to explore an exclusive interview with Ted Haggard, the megachurch pastor who stayed with his wife and started a new church after his sizzling sex scandal with a masseur.

Not your everyday churchy topic.

Craig, our national director for Lifetree Café, got a surprise message on his phone: "Don't believe Haggard or give him the time of day!" said the voice claiming to be Mike Jones. Mike Jones? *The* Mike Jones? The masseur caught in the middle of the scandal?

Craig called back to answer Mike's concerns. He explained Ted wasn't actually going to appear in person; his filmed interview would be discussed at that evening's Lifetree Café. Craig graciously invited Mike to come and participate in the discussion that night, only about an hour's drive from Mike's home.

Even though Craig thought it was improbable that Mike would actually show up, Craig encouraged Mike to represent his side of the story.

Unbeknownst to the other participants, Mike arrived and joined in at a conversation table just like the rest of the guests. After the first video segment, Mike raised his hand, faced the entire group, and declared, "I am the Mike Jones in the video."

Imagine the shock at his table as they realized they were now in conversation with the male prostitute featured in the story. But true to Lifetree fashion, they welcomed Mike into the conversation with openness and love.

The conversation unfolded. They tackled the issue of temptation and grappled with Jesus' words from the Lord's Prayer, "Lead us not into temptation." The hour included Scripture, prayer, and a lively, honest discussion.

One of the most surprising encounters occurred when a man came up to Mike afterward with a question: "How did everything that happened to you change your view of God and the church?" Some of us were holding our breath, certain that the Lifetree visitor would pounce on Mike with a biblical tirade. But no. They had a respectful conversation about the struggle with the church, while embracing God's love.

Mike hung around for almost an hour after the program talking with others. He was surprised by the nonhostile atmosphere he'd come to expect from a "Christian thing." He appreciated the dialogue and wished there was one of these cafés near him.

What's so compelling about this RADICAL HOSPITALITY? It may be because people like Mike have a preconceived idea about what Christians will do. Eighty-seven percent of people believe that Christians will be judgmental.[1] So when they experience RADICAL HOSPITALITY, it's disarming.

People who demonstrate this act of love are open to loving others without judging or looking down on them. They look past invisible differences (beliefs, attitudes, values, lifestyles, intelligence) and visible differences (clothing, skin color, age, gender, economic status). RADICAL HOSPITALITY really does welcome people just as they are.

When Jesus said, "You will be treated as you treat others" (Matthew 7:2), he was referring to the cyclical nature of our behavior toward other people. When the culture judges Christians, we judge right back. We also want the culture to know they're misjudging us—we're really not like what they think. Likewise, people outside the church think Christians are misjudging them, because *they're* not like what *we* think. Only when walls come down through relationships do both sides have a chance of coming together.

> **"DO NOT JUDGE OTHERS, AND YOU WILL NOT BE JUDGED.** For you will be treated as you treat others."
>
> —Matthew 7:1-2

The Definition of "Radical"

rad•i•cal *(adj.)*

1. Arising from or going to a root or source.
2. Departing markedly from the usual or customary; extreme.
3. Favoring or effecting fundamental or revolutionary changes in current practices, conditions, or institutions.
4. *(Slang)* Excellent; wonderful.[2]

When it comes to RADICAL HOSPITALITY, how do we define "radical"? All of the above!

JESUS' Radical Hospitality

In essence, Jesus says, "You're welcome just as you are."

Throughout his ministry, Jesus embraced the despised prostitutes, cheating tax collectors, smelly fishermen, and all manner of sinners. He reached out and touched the blind, the lame, even the "untouchables"—the lepers. Jesus opened his arms and welcomed others in such a radical way that the churchy types got pretty ticked! We humans would rather people clean up their act *before* we make connections. Thankfully, God doesn't think like that.

The New Testament is packed with unforgettable stories of Jesus' RADICAL HOSPITALITY. A favorite happened between Jesus and Zacchaeus, a notorious cheat. We love that story because it so vividly shows how religious people respond when Jesus reaches out to someone they don't think deserves it. Jesus noticed Zacchaeus, called him out, and invited himself over for dinner. The overwhelming change that happened in Zacchaeus was miraculous. And the reaction of the religious people was, well, disturbing.

61

RADICAL HOSPITALITY got Jesus into trouble because he was always hanging out, eating, and drinking with riff raff. The religious leaders frowned upon that. Didn't Jesus realize those people were "bad"? (What would the people in your church think if you found out your pastor was hanging out every Friday and Saturday night at the sleaziest bar in town?) Jesus turned everyone's world upside down—the greatest and the least.

Because *radical* means out of the ordinary, we challenge you to live love in extraordinary ways. It's strange, but today no one actually expects someone to help you, show you the way, or go above what's expected. Jesus-followers could transform the world by going the radical extra mile. We see examples of great hospitality in the everyday world around us. Like the Disney cast member who says, "Let me show you," and then escorts you there personally. Or the Starbucks barista who remembers your name and your favorite drink (even your venti extra-hot triple-shot caramel latte with no whip). In a world where we expect the least, it's radical to experience a "most."

That's the Jesus way.

All of us desperately want and need to be accepted and loved unconditionally. Don't you? So when others feel we judge them without accepting and welcoming them just as they are, they don't want to be around us. They don't get that baseline need of love and acceptance met.

Gangs, cults, and "dangerous" friends have a strong magnetic attraction. That's because people feel a sense of belonging, acceptance, and love by those groups. As dangerous and perverse as it seems, it makes sense. People will cling to anyone they feel offers a sense of belonging and acceptance. Trouble is, Jesus is the only genuine one to love us unconditionally. And we are the people called to be Jesus to others here on earth now.

Others can experience Jesus' "You're welcome just as you are" through you.

HOW TO PRACTICE LOVE
With Radical Hospitality

Acceptance doesn't mean endorsement.

You can love and accept someone without endorsing their behavior, decisions, beliefs, or lifestyle. This builds a bridge with relationships. It's unconditional love in action.

We were fascinated by a recent story of the True/False Film Fest that takes place every year in Columbia, Missouri. The co-director of the event calls himself a secular Jew, who, according to an article in *The New York Times,* is "very skeptical about American Christian culture."[3] Each year the film festival gives a major prize to honor a documentary film. The prize includes cash (sometimes in the tens of thousands of dollars) that gives financial support to the people portrayed in the documentary—usually people struggling through difficult or challenging situations.

The prize-giver? A church.

Why would an evangelical church do something crazy like that?

"We don't want to be behind a castle wall, have a moat, go out by twos to witness," said Dave Cover, the church's pastor. "We wanted to enter the culture as people who found ways to tell the story."[4]

The two don't always agree. Sometimes the films include content the conservative church disagrees with. But they work together for a common goal of connecting people in their community with stories that seek understanding about real life issues.

It's an unexpected relationship, to be sure. But because of Pastor Dave's RADICAL HOSPITALITY, it's a relationship that works. Dave knows firsthand that acceptance doesn't mean endorsement. And he's proven to at least a few of the unchurched that Christians can show love regardless of those things that tend to push us apart.

cceptance
Without Endorsement
A Travel Parable From Mongolia

Probably no country has shown us RADICAL HOSPITALITY like Mongolia. The vast, sprawling landscape gives you an idea of why hospitality is such a big deal in this culture. It can be hundreds of miles between settlements. So when travelers show up, it only makes sense that people would open their homes and offer something to eat and drink to the weary visitors.

We experienced the warmth and hospitality of the locals in some unforgettable ways. According to customs, friendly Mongolians welcome you into their round, felt, collapsible gers made for their nomadic lifestyle. By the door hangs a skin pouch filled with fermented mare's milk (from the horses). Mmmm…They fill a communal bowl that's passed from one person to the next. Imagine putting your lips to the pungent milk that tastes like a cross between sour milk, warm beer, and pickle juice.

We'll never forget passing the bowl ceremoniously from one guest to the next. (Both of us had read in the travel books: "Just touch your lips to the bowl, don't drink it.") Unfortunately, we hadn't instructed our son, Matt, on that little detail. Before we had a chance to signal to Matt, we saw him lifting the bowl and chugging it down. Bleech! *You're going to be so, so sick,* we thought. Sure enough, that night Matt was the sickest we'd ever seen him.

We love to share this story when we explain the difference between acceptance and endorsement. Traveling to Mongolia—or any other foreign culture—is like meeting others who have radically different lifestyles, actions, looks, and belief systems. We can kindly accept them (touch our lips to the mare's milk), but we don't have to endorse them (guzzle the mare's milk).

WHY NOBODY WANTS TO BE AROUND CHRISTIANS ANYMORE

> Essentially, we are sending the culture this message: Not only do we not endorse your *point of view*, we also don't accept *you*. This lack of acceptance crushes opportunities for spiritual conversations. *Acceptance* does not mean endorsement. When we confuse the two, we destroy the very space God wants to work in.[5]
>
> —Doug Pollock, *God Space*

Leave the condemning to God.

Let Scripture speak.

Condemning doesn't work. Has someone ever changed your heart or mind by condemning you first? By belittling you and what you feel, think, or do?

God knows this about us humans. He gave us the Ten Commandments to show us how to live in harmony. Honestly, if we were able to follow those laws perfectly, it'd be heaven…literally! Thanks be to Jesus who was perfect on our behalf. He came to show us love. Love sacrifices and love gives, knowing the recipient may refuse it. How do we live love like Jesus did? He went toward the suffering, needy, grieving, broken—not with condemnation—but with acceptance and love. That's magnetic!

I (Thom) experienced this firsthand recently in a radio interview I did with a popular Christian host. I explained that Jesus "led with love."

The host stopped me short. "Repent!" he shouted. "Excuse me for interrupting you, Thom. But that was Jesus' first words." He went on to defend the church's judgmental reputation as a good thing.

This man represents a widespread school of thought—that the overwhelming focal point of Scripture, of Jesus' ministry, of God, is condemnation. This view seeks to grovel in the problem, rather than embrace the solution, the grace. Yes, Jesus called us to repent, to turn from our sin. But wasn't his big purpose to love us, to call us to follow him, and to achieve something we cannot—to redeem us from our sin?

Remember, we often think of John 3:16 as the succinct summary of Jesus' mission. But the very next verse clarifies what his mission was not: "God sent his Son into the world not to judge the world, but to save the world through him" (John 3:17). So where do some get the idea that Jesus centered his ministry on condemnation? When I think of Jesus' encounters with the "unchurched" of his day, I see him leading with love and acceptance. Think of the woman caught in adultery. He led with love, defended her against those who condemned her, and then asked her to sin no more. With Zacchaeus, he led with love, accepted him, exhibited something we call RADICAL HOSPITALITY, and *then* inspired him to change his deceitful ways. With the thief on the cross beside him, Jesus led with love and invited the man to join him in paradise.

Who judged Jesus' acts of love and acceptance as unacceptable? The religious leaders, who led first with judgment. Jesus did not find their judgmental approach particularly effective either.

At a recent workshop, a religious leader approached us and said, "Okay, I hear you about this RADICAL HOSPITALITY. But when do we confront people who are living in sin?"

We explained that we're called to follow Jesus' example. Lead with love and acceptance. Once we've established a relationship, then we can invite people to dig into Scripture with us, and we can allow God to convict us and inspire each of us to turn from our sins. And thank God for the gift of forgiveness, made possible through Jesus' loving sacrifice.

The Meaning of Repentance

What does it really mean to "repent"? I always thought repentance meant me focusing on my own sins. But the Greek actually means "turn to God." It's not about groveling in my sin, but switching my focus back to God. It's not weeping in agony over my crimes; it's opening my eyes to see the outpouring of God's love for me. It's not merely about what I have done wrong, but wholeheartedly seeing what God has done.

“For God loved the world so much that he gave his one and only Son, so that everyone who believes in him will not perish but have eternal life. **GOD SENT HIS SON INTO THE WORLD NOT TO JUDGE THE WORLD, BUT TO SAVE THE WORLD THROUGH HIM.**”

—John 3:16-17

Stop looking at other people through the lens of their sins.

When we first see someone through their behavior, race, gender, sexual orientation, dress, language, tattoos, piercings, drug habits, age, looks, politics, religion, economic status...we judge. It's natural because we humans are laden with a chronic condition. It's called sin. It's ugly and keeps us from naturally seeing others like Jesus sees them.

A prime example today may be the gay issue. Every side positions itself to support its argument. Sad to say, all sides are guilty when it comes to being judgmental.

So here's a tip: When you encounter someone (a family member, neighbor, co-worker, church member, whomever), pause. Pause, take a breath, and silently talk with God about giving you the eyes and heart of Jesus.

Invite people to your place.

I (Joani) grew up on a farm in South Dakota. We always had people over. Typically we added an extra plate around the table. Our house was comfortable, which is another way of saying that sometimes it was a bit of a mess. It was lived in, but in the best way possible. Our family lived with a "throw more water in the soup" mentality. We didn't (and still don't) care about impressing people with a clean house or great furnishings. I've seen many beautiful homes that may look perfect, but at the heart they're sterile and loveless.

To this day we want our home to be an open place where people are welcome. Virtually every week we host meetings, parties, and other gatherings at our house. We recently had a party guest (a stranger before we met him that evening) who asked if he could spend the night—and, of course, we said yes! It seems that sometimes our RADICAL HOSPITALITY has no boundaries!

These days it's counter-cultural to open your home. It's risky. But inviting people into your home is one of the most practical ways of saying, "I'm inviting you into my life." Author Mike Breen talks about "life-on-life" discipleship being the only thing that can have a profound effect on people. Welcoming people into our homes may be one of the best ways of inviting people into our lives.

Our friend Nancy builds her monthly grocery list in a way that lets her "shop with hosting other people in mind, and it doesn't take so much of your time—time that you can then give to having people over." Parents who care about where their kids hang out already know this. By having food on hand, kids will congregate at your place. And you can have a profound effect on lives.

Another friend of ours, Theresa, told us about a neighborhood party her family was invited to. She and her family were a bit uncomfortable about agreeing to go because they didn't know anyone at the party. But they decided to go anyway. Once they arrived, the experience spiraled downward pretty quickly. No one introduced themselves. Everyone seemed content to chat in their existing circle of friends. Theresa's family sat and ate in awkward silence while everyone else partied on. Finally, after an hour or so, the host invited them to join in a game. At last, someone welcomed them, reached out, and included them.

Theresa and I talked about RADICAL HOSPITALITY and the importance of being in tune with how others may be feeling. As Christians, let's take the lead in making others feel genuinely welcome, whether it's in our homes, our workplaces, our schools, or our churches. We need to look outside ourselves and treat others as we would want to be treated.

> "When I am with those who are weak, I share their weakness, for I want to bring the weak to Christ. Yes, **I TRY TO FIND COMMON GROUND WITH EVERYONE, DOING EVERYTHING I CAN TO SAVE SOME.**"
>
> —1 Corinthians 9:22

Be profoundly relational.

We heard of an elderly woman, Fern, who lived in a house that butted up against a high school. Her blood boiled as she watched a gang of smokers hang out by her backyard, leaving trash and cigarette butts in her yard. Instead of lashing out with anger, getting law enforcement involved, or taking her complaint to the school board, she applied some RADICAL HOSPITALITY. She bought a loaf of bread and some peanut butter and jelly and reached out to the tough kids. She took the time to get to know the kids, welcome them unconditionally, and love them. After earning the right to speak into their lives, she hoped some would stop smoking, at least for their own health benefits. But the kids knew Fern cared. She became their "grandma." Soon the kids were cleaning up Fern's yard, helping her with chores, and falling in love with Fern!

Imagine what might have happened if Fern had chosen not to show RADICAL HOSPITALITY. Nothing good, that's for certain. Were the kids in the wrong? Sure. Would Fern have been justified in responding angrily? Most would say yes. But RADICAL HOSPITALITY sees the mess, sees the challenge, sees the ugly…and loves anyway. Fern chose to forge and nurture a relationship rather than be right or be the victim. RADICAL HOSPITALITY looks for opportunities—sometimes the most difficult opportunities—and finds a way to love.

Seek to understand.

Jean was active in her church, sang in the praise band, and volunteered for lots of things. So it was a surprise when Jean suddenly stopped coming to church. The active church members were miffed. She was shirking her duties. One afternoon Jean stopped by the church to pick up some mail. She ran into Ginger, who suppressed her judgmental tone and asked, "Where have you been? We missed you." Jean took a deep breath and said, "I got a divorce. I didn't think I was welcome here anymore." Ginger wrapped her arms around her and said, "Oh, Jean, you're always welcome here!" Tearing up and heartbroken, Jean replied in a whisper, "Thank you, I'll be back."

It is so easy to judge. But there's always more to the story—truths that lie below the surface or in the shadows. Most often we form our opinion like the church members who thought Jean was being irresponsible and lazy. After learning the rest of the story about what Jean had been going through, they were not so quick to judge.

Expect opportunities to show RADICAL HOSPITALITY.

Our friend for decades, Jeanne lives an expectant life, ready for hospitality. To remind her of the person she will welcome at any time, she puts a lovely, seasonal place-setting on her kitchen counter. Even though the mystery guest is unlikely and usually unknown, the place-setting is a daily reminder of opening her heart to others. Jeanne says, "It's my morning visual on how to live my day."

It's likely that every day presents an opportunity for you to practice RADICAL HOSPITALITY to someone with whom you cross paths. There is no shortage of people who could use the gift of a caring, welcoming person in their life. How awesome would it be if, in a time of need, the first thing people would say is, "I need a Christian!" If you expect to be that person, you'll be surprised at how often the opportunities come along for you to show love through RADICAL HOSPITALITY.

Let people know you're thinking of them.

Jeanne doesn't only set the table for the possibility of showing RADICAL HOSPITALITY; she actively sends cards, emails, or text messages to people when they come to mind. To accommodate her out-of-the-blue prompts, she keeps a pack of homemade cards and stamps on hand. I (Joani) also keep a ready stash of note cards (sometimes Thom's photos-turned-cards) at our kitchen desk to send caring messages. Just keeping note cards on hand can remind you to send that radical rarity—a handwritten note. I've never met anyone who doesn't cherish getting a personal note of encouragement from someone they know. It's always powerful, and it's always welcome—just like God's never-ending love.

Practice the healing power of touch.

Give hugs! You may be surprised by how many people appreciate a hug. I (Joani) am a generous hugger. Thom wonders if I give off some kind of hug radar to people around me—they seem to sense I will embrace them. We raised our son, Matt, to be a happy hugger, too. Every month during our all-staff meeting at Group, we (yes, Thom too!) hug our staff members who are celebrating anniversaries that month. That may seem odd to think a company would hug to honor long-timers, but we believe there's healing power in touch. Hugs are a mini-celebration of our relationships.

We believe positive touch has been eliminated in our culture because of fear. Of course, horrific things have happened in people's lives when trust and touch have been abused. However, to cast aside the gift of physical touch takes away one of the essential gifts God has given humanity. Perhaps it will help if we all practice three safe standards for the hug: Keep it proper, keep it public, and keep it pure.

Our friends Art and Nancy told us a heartwarming story of Art's mom, Anna Louise, in her final years. Throughout her life she loved to talk. She especially liked talking about the love of Jesus. Sadly, as her health declined, she lost her ability to speak. However, nothing could keep her from church and showing others Jesus' love. During the portion of the worship service when people were invited to greet each other and share "the peace of Christ," Anna Louise would go from person to person, cradle their face, and kiss their cheeks. At her funeral, the pastor said, "Anna Louise changed our church." Now people freely greet their friends with a "holy kiss," Anna Louise–style. She transformed a congregation without ever saying a word!

Unconditional love takes time, so be patient.

In an age of instant everything, remember that RADICAL HOSPITALITY takes time. Be willing to invest in someone's life for the long haul. When you embrace the idea that "you're welcome just as you are," that means trusting God's timing. Just as it takes time for a tree to grow, for any masterpiece to be created, relationships developed through RADICAL HOSPITALITY need to marinate in love for a long time.

During one of our mission trips to India, we met an Indian pastor with a heart for the snake charmer community. (We never knew snake-charmer communities existed!) These groups attract those who believe the cobra is a god. You've probably seen (in cartoons, at least) an Indian wearing a turban, sitting cross-legged, playing a horn that intoxicatingly beckons a cobra to point its head toward you. We learned Indians believe the cobra god will bless or curse your home depending on if you pay the snake charmer. So snake charmers go from dwelling to dwelling using the cobra as their means of livelihood.

Do you know how many years the local pastor has shown his unconditional love and acceptance to this community? *Seven years so far!* Without one convert. Talk about patience and simply showing love to those people. We were humbled by his heart and realized how impatient we tend to be, even with matters of faith. After our visit, one elder of the village said to the pastor, "Your God must be very important to send these foreigners to this place." Yes, our God is so filled with love for the world "that he gave his one and only Son, so that everyone who believes in him will not perish but have eternal life. God sent his Son into the world not to judge the world, but to save the world through him" (John 3:16-17).

Be consistent.

Consistency builds trust. RADICAL HOSPITALITY means I can count on you, time and time again, to do what you said you'd do.

We all know people who tend to be unpredictable. They tend to be the kind of person who, if you're meeting them for lunch, you think to yourself, *I hope they're in a good mood.* In other words, you're never sure how this person is going to treat you. You never know if they'll be mad or glad or somewhere else on the emotional roller coaster. It's disconcerting to be in a relationship with someone who treats you erratically. For Christians, others look to us to be steadfast in our character and our beliefs.

We interviewed a brilliant young professor, Holly Ordway, who was once an atheist and is now a Jesus-follower. Her journey to discover faith involved a fervent intellectual quest for truth. But there was something that struck her about one of the Christians she knew. Her fencing coach was a talented, brilliant, caring man who never forced his Christian faith on Holly. For years, she watched her coach live his faith gently, authentically, and consistently in Jesus-style love. He was one of the God-timed relationships that embraced Holly's questions and showed her the power of a life in Christ.

RADICAL HOSPITALITY can happen online, too.

Our friend and co-worker Brian told us about a time he was on staff at a church in Wisconsin, stumped as to how to connect with university students. One night, out of sheer frustration, he asked God to inspire him with ideas. Not surprisingly, the ideas flowed.

Although he didn't have an Xbox, he knew that a lot of students spent their time online playing video games. With the release of the new *Halo 2* game coming out the next week, Brian bought an Xbox and started a new faith and gaming community on the Internet. He called it Xbox Mission. But he didn't know what to expect.

It turned out that a lot of gamers believe in God too. His forum became one of the largest online faith communities for gamers, thriving as a place for young people to build relationships with other Christians. They encouraged each other, prayed together, and played games multiple times a week. Though they were sometimes met with jeers from curious outsiders, Brian said they worked hard to maintain a culture of friendliness and respect. They were even challenged to games by players claiming to be satanists and atheists, yet they kept their focus on building relationships and showing respect to everyone. Eventually, many of those connections turned into close friendships outside of cyberspace.

"It was one of the craziest times in my faith. It challenged me to rethink how I interacted with people and where I was willing to go," Brian said.

Although it's become a place for "trolls" to thrive in anonymous nastiness, the Internet provides tremendous opportunities for Christians to be salt and light. Treat people online with the same courtesy and respect that you'd give your best friend. Even though you can't see someone, even though you can be virtually anonymous, you can still be a Christian example of RADICAL HOSPITALITY. Imagine them face to face, friend to friend, and you can show a Jesus-style love that's just as powerful as if they were literally in front of you.

Use the power of names...with care.

Research has proven what we already know: We love to hear other people say our names. Encouraging words—coupled with our names—carries so much weight.

Of course, just the sound of our names isn't enough. We prefer to hear our names spoken in love. We tried an experiment with children's workers, where we had a small group use each other's names first in anger, then in frustration, then using a mocking tone, and finally in love. Even though everyone knew it was a simulated activity (pretend), it had a profound effect. It hurt to hear our names spoken in any unloving tone. If you're a parent, a co-worker, a teacher, or a supervisor, know that it matters *how* you speak someone's name.

The old saying "sticks and stones may break my bones, but words will never hurt me" is not true. Words hold extreme power, both for good and bad. That's why calling each other "names" is not only hurtful, it's dangerous. In our youth ministry days, we had a ground rule: No put-downs.

For years we've led a simple experience (with all ages) using a piece of paper in the shape of a person. We ask participants to pass the paper person around the circle. Each time they receive it, they think of a time they've heard or said something that's mean, hurtful, and tears down another person. As they speak, they rip the paper. Bit by bit, the paper person gets demolished. Then together we read Ephesians 4:29: "Don't use foul or abusive language. Let everything you say be good and helpful, so that your words will be an encouragement to those who hear them." Next, they take turns sharing a time they heard or said a kind or encouraging word that lifted someone up. As they speak, they tape the paper person back together. The positive power of words puts those figures back together. The experience is a powerful metaphor of what happens to real people in real life.

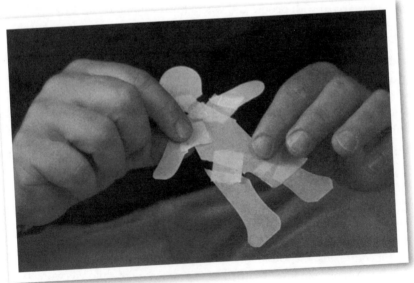

Remember our names hold spiritual power, too. God says, "I have called you by name; you are mine" (Isaiah 43:1).

WHY NOBODY WANTS TO BE AROUND CHRISTIANS ANYMORE

Forgive.

Alicia Brady was a talented young lady who dreamed of being a dancer. Her whole life revolved around her dream. She'd practiced ballet since age 9, and she looked forward to a lifetime filled with dance on a professional level. But one fateful night after a party in a sketchy neighborhood, a shooter mistakenly aimed at her friend's car. A shot rang out. She felt a warm, bloody pain in her stomach. Alicia had been shot. In an instant, she was paralyzed. She spent years in physical therapy…years wondering… and years hating an unidentified gunman. Her dreams of being a dancer had been dashed.

But her story didn't end there. Instead of drinking the poison of unforgiveness, Alicia forgave the shooter—even though she didn't know the man. On top of that, she decided to volunteer in a prison. Today, Alicia is healed in more ways than one. God gave her an opportunity. A different young shooter had the chance to tell her he was sorry. He never got to tell his dead victim that. Alicia graciously offered to forgive that man as if he were her shooter.

RADICAL HOSPITALITY—welcoming others just as they are— sometimes means forgiving the person you need to love. Sometimes again and again. In not forgiving, you're drinking the poison you hope will destroy the other person, and in reality, you're destroying any opportunity you may ever have to make your faith magnetic. Forgiveness is an act of love in itself. And the great thing about it? God gives you the power to forgive. You never have to do it on your own strength.

> "Make allowances for each other's faults, and forgive anyone who offends you. **REMEMBER, THE LORD FORGAVE YOU, SO YOU MUST FORGIVE OTHERS.**"
>
> —Colossians 3:13

Be okay with messy.

You know what? Relationships can be messy. Living in the mess can feel frustrating, tedious, disappointing. And usually we don't even know where to begin to clean things up.

We have been blessed to have been befriended by so many people—far more than our fair share. But it's a gift that comes with its share of difficulties. We've learned everyone has a story of disorder and muck somewhere in the relationships in their lives. If we take the time to be profoundly relational, we can find the courage it takes to be radically hospitable. We have to let others into our lives so we can get into theirs. They're all going to happen—the family squabbles, work conflicts, community struggles, illness, church politics, neighbor fights, (fill in yours here: _____). There is no shortage of mess, and the mess is inevitable.

Embrace it! If there's one thing we've learned about loving relationships, it's that they're always worth it. And we're not in heaven yet.

Expect surprises.

Shawna told us about one cold morning when she was busy in the kitchen making a latte with the last of her espresso. She glanced outside and saw the man next door scooping the last shovel of snow from her driveway. How kind! So instead of enjoying that latte herself, she dashed to the helpful neighbor's front door, latte in hand. Her neighbor wasn't expecting anything, but one act of RADICAL HOSPITALITY spawned another. And another, as Shawna and Matt, her husband, were inspired to shovel someone else's driveway. RADICAL HOSPITALITY is beginning to revolutionize their neighborhood!

RADICAL HOSPITALITY surprises people. We can view things like snow and ice as unwelcome hassles. Or we can see them as opportunities to show Jesus' love.

Our friend Cris shared a similar story with us about her neighbor who simply surprised her family with a chicken pot pie the week her husband was out of town. Surprises don't need to be huge. They can come in the form of raking leaves, carrying in a grocery load, offering to watch the kids, volunteering to run an errand, maybe even offering a listening ear.

If Christians became known for this one thing—surprising people with acts of RADICAL HOSPITALITY—our reputation would change almost overnight.

Prepare for disappointment.

When you give of yourself freely to others, sometimes you might be disappointed. Sometimes you might be taken advantage of. You might even get hurt.

Never let it stop you.

Each year Group hosts a Community Service Awards banquet to celebrate all the nonprofit work in our backyard of northern Colorado. Each year more than 100 organizations apply to receive grants that come from Group's annual profits. It's one of our favorite days of the year! Our staff organizes the event and chooses the recipients after much deliberation and prayer.

One particular year, the team chose the grand prize recipient: a thriving biker church in our town. Many bikers who'd never known Jesus were coming to this church and growing in faith and service. It was an awesome ministry! We presented the pastor of the church with a giant check for $25,000, and the inspiring event was reported in the local paper.

To our shock, we found out a few weeks later that the pastor had absconded with the money and left the biker church in the lurch.

Our team had done their due diligence and handled everything properly, but we couldn't control one man's greed. Our world is broken. But we're happy to say that theft didn't stop us from loving the community again and again. In fact, so far our gifts to the local community have topped a million dollars!

When God has been so good to us, we want to share his goodness. Even though we might get hurt, we can turn those disappointments into teachable moments. We risk it because it's worth it.

One time a pastor friend of ours told us that close relationships weren't worth the pain. He said they were like getting one paper cut after another. We thought that was indescribably sad. Yes, there's pain, but we can't imagine a world in which the effort of loving others wasn't worth it.

We're blessed to be able to work with wonderful people, most of whom become our friends. As so often happens in life, though, circumstances arise that cause conflict. Sometimes members of our team make poor decisions that disappoint us. I (Thom) actually turned disappointments into a class for leaders at Group to help prepare them for the possibility of disappointment. I call it "Skeletons in the Closet." I have a small cupboard full of small plastic skeletons wearing toe tags. Out of respect for those involved, no names are named, but each skeleton represents a real-life example of someone who is no longer working at Group. Each chose to do something disappointing that led to that person's dismissal. We use this small cupboard and its contents only to teach our leaders about disappointment and how to forgive and let it go.

People will disappoint you in life. Yet, through all disappointment, we choose to love. Again and again. Paper cut after paper cut. The deep well of God's love never runs dry, and we are compelled to dip our cups as often as we can.

Be a friend, even when it's not your job.

People have built-in radar to detect if someone's sincerely interested in them or not. This is precisely why we let friends at Lifetree Café know they can hang around as long as they like. And they do—often up to an hour after the program has officially ended. It's during this "After Words" period that people follow up on conversations sparked earlier and dig deeper into what's important to them.

I (Joani) encountered a great example of this kind of RADICAL HOSPITALITY on one of my "Jeanne Joani Journeys." My long-time friend Jeanne and I scoured the local listings and Internet for a church to visit one Sunday while we were traveling together. After we found one, here's what transpired when we got there:

We were greeted at the door by a smiling woman who said, "I don't think I've met you before." We proceeded to explain we were visiting and enjoying one of our favorite things to do as friends—our "JJJs" (Jeanne Joani Journeys). She comfortably engaged in small talk, and then pointed us toward the fellowship room for coffee and treats. With a glimmer in her eye, she said, "You can take your coffee into the sanctuary. We weren't always able to do that, but we changed the rules. We can now!" With a smile and a nod, she passed us on to another woman near the fellowship room door who further welcomed us in and made sure we were taken care of.

Once in the sanctuary, another woman turned around, leaned over the pew, and greeted us. She wasn't "on duty." She was part of a naturally hospitable church. We felt very welcome in this family of believers.

Be daringly, caringly curious.

Rick, our friend and co-worker, is genius at this. He has a knack of asking "one more question." It really is fun to watch. The act of fully engaged, face-to-face conversation is becoming a lost art. Yet diving deep into people's stories is like scuba diving to find treasure. You don't know what you'll find, but it will be a worthwhile adventure.

We love Bob Goff's book *Love Does*. His over-the-top, radical approach to love bubbles out of him. And it's real. He got raised eyebrows when he gave his phone number in his book to welcome phone calls to prove his love anytime, anywhere philosophy. We interviewed him about his book and his approach to life. And yes, his phone went off during the middle of the interview. Right then and there, Bob answered his phone, greeted the unknown caller enthusiastically, and shared he'd call back since he was in the middle of a video interview. He just proved to us how serious he was about having fun with *Love Does*. We highly recommend his book for a chance to read how RADICAL HOSPITALITY shows up in one man's life.

Warning: Technology is changing relationships.

When I ask people 'What's wrong with having a conversation?' People say, 'I'll tell you what's wrong with having a conversation. It takes place in real time and you can't control what you're going to say.' So that's the bottom line. Texting, email, posting, all of these thing let us present the self as we want to be. We get to edit, and that means we get to delete, and that means we get to retouch, the face, the voice, the flesh, the body—not too little, not too much, just right.

Human relationships are rich and they're messy and they're demanding. And we clean them up with technology. And when we do, one of the things that can happen is that we sacrifice conversation for mere connection. We short-change ourselves.[6]

—Sherry Turkle, author of *Alone Together*

We don't like to put hands and feet on love. When love is a theory, it's safe, it's free of risk. But love in the brain changes nothing...[L]ove is too beautiful a concept to keep locked up behind a forehead like a prisoner... [Real] *love does* things.[7]

—Donald Miller, from the foreword
of *Love Does* by Bob Goff

Just smile.

Your smile is a gift. Not only does it convey warmth and the very beginnings of RADICAL HOSPITALITY, it also makes *you* feel better. It's like they say, "If you have the joy of the Lord, tell your face."

A study published in the journal *Psychological Science* "confirms the benefits of the warm gesture: When pedestrians on a busy street walk past a stranger who smiled at them, they felt more connected to others."[8]

Eat together.

There's more power in sharing a meal than you may realize. A Gallup survey explored the link between friendship and faith, and the research revealed that church attendees who share meals together experience higher church satisfaction. In fact, those who eat meals together are three times more likely to say they're highly satisfied with their church.[9]

In their book *Many Tables*, Dennis E. Smith and Hal E. Taussig write, "In the New Testament, it is notable that Jesus is defined as a 'friend of tax collectors and sinners' precisely by his act of dining with them."[10] Pharisees and teachers of the law were often caught muttering, "This man welcomes sinners and eats with them" (Luke 15:2).

The authors call it "banquet friendship," which resulted when people left behind "the divisive social rankings of outer society and in effect [formed] a new society with new social rules."[11] Jesus rocked cultural barriers simply by eating with others.

In his book *The Friendship Factor*, Alan Loy McGinnis writes, "There is something almost sacramental about breaking bread with another and it is almost impossible to have dinner with an enemy and remain enemies."[12]

By sharing food, you can break down social barriers to create common experiences that "form a new society." Bring on the potlucks, barbeques, snacks, and desserts. Try home dinner groups, dinner-and-a-movie nights, and coffee shop get-togethers. Plan a neighborhood get-together. Meet at restaurants. Capitalize on heightened interest in cooking shows and exotic foods. Enlist the foodies in your midst to show all the RADICAL HOSPITALITY they can cook up. *Bon appétit!*

Go out of your way to say something.

Extroverts will love this. Introverts not so much. But it's powerful, nonetheless. If you go out of your way to strike up a conversation, you've just started something truly extraordinary. Faith is a relationship, and relationships talk.

Chitchat is never a waste of time. It's a critical time in a relationship when you're getting comfortable with each other, searching for common ground. With a little bit of insight and some keen listening, chitchat brings us closer to strangers quickly and effectively. Think of it as a social lubricant. Those small conversations about the weather are often a first step toward full-on RADICAL HOSPITALITY.

Befriend the hard to love, those who believe they're far from God.

Our experiment with Lifetree Café has opened us up to hundreds of people we would have never crossed paths with. It's been nothing short of a miracle to be part of a place that provides often the only listening hearts and ears people can find in our community. Week after week, curious, hopeful, and hurting people walk through our doors, and we get the chance to "glow" Jesus into their lives. We believe that's something only God can do.

In all honesty, it's not easy. We've met and befriended many people who are struggling in ways we had never imagined possible. These are people who say they have nowhere else to turn—no family, no loved ones, no church, no one. Yet they find the help, encouragement, and love—the RADICAL HOSPITALITY—they desperately need at Lifetree Café. We've shed tears with them, stayed up late with them, and, truth be told, sometimes spent moments a little afraid of them. But we've always looked to God for the strength and courage we need to be Jesus to those people.

We've come to realize what's happening: Our team's RADICAL HOSPITALITY is making our faith in Jesus magnetic.

When in doubt, let love find a way.

It's tempting to slip back into our old habits of judging first, asking questions later. Sometimes you may feel yourself facing a situation that seems to demand more of you than you're willing to give. Perhaps you've become good friends with a woman, only to be surprised by an invitation to her lesbian wedding. Or you've spent months mentoring a young person in your neighborhood, only to be surprised by their admission that they just can't get past their doubts about God. Your RADICAL HOSPITALITY

81

("I care about you, and you're always welcome in my life") shows them that you love them no matter what. No, it's not easy. But it is necessary. That's what God does with each of us. His heart and his arms are wide open to us despite our doubts, shortcomings, failures, mistakes, and baggage.

Love can always find a way.

Phew!

That's the tip of the relational iceberg. You can spend the rest of your life practicing fresh new ways to love others with RADICAL HOSPITALITY. Our hearts have changed and so can yours. And your faith will grow more magnetic with every simple act.

But that's only the first of the 4 ACTS OF LOVE. Next up: FEARLESS CONVERSATION.

Endnotes

1. David Kinnaman and Gabe Lyons, *UnChristian* (Grand Rapids, MI: Baker Books, 2007), 27.

2. The American Heritage Dictionary of the English Language, Fourth Edition. S.v. "radical." http://www.thefreedictionary.com/radical.

3. Lauren Sandler, "Crossing a Divide, Seeking Good," New York Times, February 21, 2014, http://www.nytimes.com/2014/02/23/movies/how-the-true-false-film-festival-and-a-church-work-together.html.

4. Ibid.

5. Doug Pollock, *God Space* (Loveland, CO: Group Publishing, 2009), 31.

6. Sherry Turkle, "Connected, but alone?" talk given at TED 2012 Conference, February 2012, http://www.ted.com/talks/sherry_turkle_alone_together/transcript.

7. Donald Miller, foreword to *Love Does: Discover a Secretly Incredible Life in an Ordinary World*, by Bob Goff (Nashville, TN: Thomas Nelson, 2012), x-xi.

8. First for Women, "The power of a single smile," October 1, 2012, 50.

9. Group Publishing, *Friendship: Creating a Culture of Connectivity in Your Church* (Loveland, CO: Group Publishing, 2005), 11.

10. Dennis E. Smith and Hal E. Taussig, *Many Tables: The Eucharist in the New Testament and Liturgy Today* (Philadelphia, PA: Trinity Press International, 1990), 31.

11. Ibid., 34.

12. Alan Loy McGinnis, *The Friendship Factor* (Minneapolis, MN: Augsburg Fortress, 2004), 53.

5

FEARLESS CONVERSATION

> "Sure, I'll talk to you. **AS LONG AS YOU'RE REALLY WILLING TO HEAR WHY** I don't go to church anymore."

And so the FEARLESS CONVERSATION began.

I (Joani) sat down for coffee with Chris, a cheerful 40-something-year-old guy who looked like he could be friends with anyone. I had sent out a request for personal stories from anyone who could shed some light for this book we were beginning to write—*Why Nobody Wants to Be Around Christians Anymore.* The stories poured in (not to my surprise), and so many of them broke my heart. Chris was one who agreed to sit down with me, but his apprehension was darker than the cup of coffee clenched between my hands. It was clear he didn't trust Christians, and I was eager to discover why.

We'd never chatted before, but I told him I was thrilled that he was willing to take time to share his story with me. We caught up with small talk—the usual stuff like weather, the roads, and his job. (Never underestimate the importance of small talk, by the way. It's a great way to break the ice and get comfortable with each other.)

Once we were settled in (and the coffee was still hot), I mentioned our book project to him. Then I opened it up for him to share. "So, I'm curious. What's your story?" I asked.

I leaned forward and wasn't afraid to ask him to open up the raw, painful secrets of his past. (You'd be surprised how willing people are to share about themselves to someone who's genuinely interested. I certainly was.)

Chris jumped right in and told me why he doesn't go to church. It had been a long, long time—he hadn't been to church since he was a young boy. Here's what he told me:

"I remember when I was 9 or 10 years old. It was a long time ago. My neighbor friend, Jason, invited me to go to church with him on Wednesday night. He said it'd be fun. So I thought that'd be okay. My family didn't go to church, but I thought I'd go with my friend. We got to the church, and they had cookies and stuff. We went downstairs to the church basement and gathered around a table."

My childhood memories of my own little church's musty basement came rushing back to me. It was easy for me to identify with Chris. (It's always great to empathize as much as you can when others share their story. It shows you understand who they are and where they're coming from.)

"The teacher passed out a pamphlet with pictures and started telling us about Jesus. She said he came to earth to die on a cross and to save us from our sins."

Chris said his hand shot up. "I don't get it," the young Chris asked. "What do you mean 'sins'?"

"I'm 9 or 10, and I'm thinking, 'Sins, what sins?' The teacher glared at me." Chris re-enacted his entire experience as we talked. I marveled at how well he remembered all the details.

"Then the teacher said, 'Jesus died on a cross for you.' My hand shot up again. 'I don't get it,' I said. 'You mean some dude 2,000 years ago died for *me?*' And the teacher glared at me again. I could tell she was really irritated at me. Then she said the most outrageous thing of all. She said Jesus died and came back from the dead three days later. 'Whaaaat?' I said again, raising my hand. 'Hey, like I watch cable and stuff. So Jesus was a zombie?'"

Chris's story grabbed me by the heart, and I could tell it wasn't going to end well. It was all too easy for me to picture this scenario. By this time, the exasperated teacher had all she could take from this little "punk." He was interrupting her lesson plans. He was asking questions she deemed silly. He wasn't taking it seriously. In her mind, he was nothing but a troublemaker who only wanted to cause havoc in her class. And if he kept it up, she'd never get through her lesson plans. So the teacher did what she felt she had to do.

She told Chris to shut up.

"So I did," Chris said. He crossed his arms, sat back in his chair, and thought, "I'm done with this."

As he and Jason loaded into the red station wagon, Jason's mother glowered at Chris and slammed the car door shut. "What did you do in there?" she shouted. "The teacher told me you were so disruptive, she never wants to see you back again!"

Chris said he was shocked at Jason's mom's outrage. It hit him harder than if it had come from his own mother. He had no idea what he could have done that was so horrible.

Well, the teacher got what she wished for.

Chris hasn't been back to church for decades, and his anger, frustration, and disgust are still palpable to this day. He said that one experience skewed his view of Christians. He sees religion as something that's all about power and control, not love.

Sadly, we hear stories like Chris's all the time. We've even talked with 70-year-olds who had been kicked out of Sunday school as a child because they asked too many questions. And they never went back.

As hard as it was to hear, I loved my conversation with Chris. It was a healthy two-way dialogue and very respectful. I admitted to him that I didn't have all the answers, and I even admitted that I had a lot of questions myself. (He liked that a lot.) After an hour and a half, we left as friends. He's even open to joining us for some of our events, now that he understands we're not "those typical Christians."

One thing Chris said really stuck with me. He's a musician, and he used a stereo to illustrate his point. Stereos have two speakers—a left side and a right side. When you play the music out of only one speaker, you don't get the full sound. Chris said we need both sides—both voices—to get the full sound. The *better* sound. What a profound illustration of what FEARLESS CONVERSATIONS are all about.

Lessons **LEARNED**

Chris's story demonstrates FEARLESS CONVERSATION on many levels:

1. I invited the conversation. And Chris was willing to talk. Amazingly, in all our work with the unchurched and the dechurched, no one has ever turned us down when invited to share their story. When done in love, they are thankful and eager to have a dialogue.

2. The church teacher seemed afraid of having an open conversation with that curious little 9-year-old. We Christians should have nothing to fear. "Fear not!" Remember?

3. Questions are good. Read the Gospels and highlight all the questions Jesus asked. You'll be surprised how often Jesus asked probing, open-ended questions. He was the Master Asker.

4. When it comes to spiritual things, FEARLESS CONVERSATIONS are like a fertile garden where faith (a relationship, remember) can really grow.

Chris and I had a fearless yet safe conversation that allowed us both to be completely honest with each other. I had no agenda other than to listen. There was no way I was going to undo 30-plus years of damage in one hour over coffee. I didn't need to persuade him of anything. I simply wanted to become his friend.

"Your thoughts are welcome. Your doubts are welcome."

Imagine Jesus saying that. Jesus was never afraid to talk, never afraid to listen to anyone's comments, never afraid to hear the doubts so many people had.

When we hear the story of Thomas doubting Jesus, we always assume Jesus was upset by his doubt. But take a closer look. Jesus responded only by asking, "Why are you frightened? Why are your hearts filled with doubt?" (Luke 24:38).

What if Jesus was simply lovingly confronting Thomas, wanting to know what was going on in his mind?

Imagine Jesus saying, *Okay, you have doubts and questions? Then "look at my hands. Look at my feet. You can see that it's really me. Touch me and make sure that I am not a ghost, because ghosts don't have bodies, as you see that I do"* (Luke 24:39).

We, too, can show our hands and feet—our everyday lives—to those with doubts and questions. Let's assure them through our own stories and experiences that Jesus is real. That's an act of love. That's another way we can make our faith magnetic.

People want freedom to ask, wonder, and experience give and take. Jesus gave his friends something to hold on to in the midst of their doubts. You can give them *you*—your listening ear, gentle touch, and open mind—so they can see Jesus alive in you. What an awesome privilege to be given the same opportunity as the risen Christ.

86

> **"I also pray that you will understand the incredible greatness of God's power for us who believe him. THIS IS THE SAME MIGHTY POWER THAT RAISED CHRIST FROM THE DEAD AND SEATED HIM IN THE PLACE OF HONOR AT GOD'S RIGHT HAND IN THE HEAVENLY REALMS."** —Ephesians 1:19-20

As Christians, we feel an obligation to share the Gospel, and many believers have been trained to be blunt and ambitious in telling others about how Jesus can save their souls. But there are some important things to remember for Christians eager to speak the good news:

- **Welcome questions, and don't feel like you have to have the answers to all of them.** People of all ages have legitimate questions, and like it or not, Christians don't always have easy answers. No question should be off-limits. No question is too dumb. In Chris's case, he was responding honestly when he heard the incredible story of salvation. We shouldn't be surprised when others want to grapple with the remarkable account of God sending his Son to die for us, conquer death, and come back to life.

- **Don't assume people's motives when they ask questions.** Instead of getting defensive, try to see the other person as Jesus sees them. It's very unlikely that they're out to sabotage you and break you down. Fear not. God is with you. There's no reason to feel threatened or insecure. Your only job is to love, so let God do the rest of the work.

- **Let go of your agenda. Your script or lesson plan isn't the answer.** A friend told us about a time she went to a Bible study. She raised her hand because she wanted to share how God had spoken to her through one of the Scriptures that was part of the study. The teacher snapped at her. "We don't have time for that. Maybe if we have time at the end of the class you can share." Of course, our friend never got to share her personal encounter with God. How much do we miss when we stick to our agenda rather than letting God show up?

87

"You just lecture me."

Many non-churchgoers say, "You Christians just lecture me. You don't care what I think." They would never expect us to tell them that we welcome their thoughts and their doubts. And because of this kind of Christian behavior, they never expect that from Jesus either. Yet Jesus was always curious about what people thought. Time and time again throughout the Gospels, he asked what people thought…and he listened. There's a good reason Jesus never came to be known as "The Great Lecturer."

Hearing what other people think opens the door for God to work. "Wait…what? You actually care about me and what I think? Hmm. Maybe I'll listen to what you have to say, since you've shown me honor by caring about me first."

For Jesus, no conversation was off limits. Prostitutes. Sick people. Possessed people. Friends. An unproductive fig tree. The wind and waves. Disgruntled church people. Even a feisty encounter with the devil. Jesus was confident of the power that was in him: God's power.

That same power will help us with our FEARLESS CONVERSATIONS.

As Christians, we seem to forget that God is on our side. He's with us. He'll never leave us or forsake us. We simply need to be faithful and trust him. He'll give us the words to say—or not to say. Too often Christians think that overpowering others with the Bible yields results. Yet FEARLESS CONVERSATION is, by definition, engaging without fear. Engaging with love.

 Travel Parable
From the Shark Cage

We've done a lot of wild things: Tornado chasing. Visiting cannibals. Hiking exploding volcanoes. Crossing the Drake Passage (known as the most treacherous seas in the world) to Antarctica. Piloting over glaciers in Alaska. Scuba diving in WWII Japanese shipwrecks. Eating lap-lap, the national dish of Vanuatu. Some would say these adventures are crazy and insane. We, however, like to think of them as calculated risks. Exciting, but not deadly.

One particular adventure taught me (Joani) a lot about fear: shark cage diving. We planned to encounter great white sharks in one of the few places on the planet where you can do such things: near Cape Town, South Africa.

Now, there are TV shows and weeks dedicated to the wonders and dangers of sharks. The great whites are gnarly, mean, and nasty looking! We know. We stared them in the face within inches. They're creepy looking, scary, fierce, daunting, scarred, and grisly.

We loaded onto a boat equipped with a steel cage able to hold a couple humans hanging overboard and a fake wooden seal. (I wouldn't have been fooled by the floppy decoy, but the sharks were.) We aimed for a spot close to an island covered with seals—barking, sniffing, smelly seals. They are the reason great whites like to hang out here. They're a scrumptious breakfast, lunch, or dinner for a hungry shark.

The captain briefed us on the procedures for the shark cage dive. I didn't feel too reassured when I noticed he was missing a few fingers. Gulp! Our mission: Don your snorkel mask, jump into the cage over the side of the boat, go underwater when the captain yells, "Down! Down! Down!" and take a giant gulp of air, so you can hold your breath as the sharks take aim at the cage. The experience was surreal. The giant monsters slammed toward the steel bars of the cage, glaring at us as they swarmed around the cage.

All this sounds terrifying. But here's the truth: We were safe and secure behind those bars. The experience lasted as long as we could hold our breath. We had a captain who'd done this hundreds of times before. We were safe even though it looked like we were facing a death-defying moment.

It was exhilarating!

This example reminds us of FEARLESS CONVERSATIONS. Christians work themselves into a tizzy, scared to death of actually talking with someone who holds a different opinion. Somehow we're sure we won't emerge unscathed. We fear we'll be eaten alive. We don't trust our guide who's been there before. We imagine we're all alone with the sharks. We forget our captain—our Captain—will be with us.

And we forget how exhilarating a fearless faith conversation can be when we experience God in action. Fear not!

How to **PRACTICE LOVE**
Through Fearless Conversation

People don't want to be lectured to, but they do want to talk. They don't want to be condescended to by know-it-all believers, but they crave a fair, meaningful dialogue. They don't want to be corrected and preached at by their Christian friends, but they will always be open to having a FEARLESS CONVERSATION with them.

Remember, as Christians our goal is not to go out there and "fix" every unchurched person we meet. That's God's job, not ours. Our goal is to show love.

The rest of this chapter will show you practical, natural ways of loving others with FEARLESS CONVERSATION. These are things we've learned over the last few years, and we can tell you from personal experience that every principle and tip works. We've watched them happen again and again and heard countless stories from those who've engaged in FEARLESS CONVERSATION. It's a truly remarkable act of love, and the more you do it, the more magnetic your faith will become.

Love first, always.

It should go without saying, but we feel compelled to start with the *most essential ingredient* for FEARLESS CONVERSATION: love, pure and simple. It's the kind of love, exhibited even when we disagree, that Jesus called us to pursue: "Love each other. Just as I have loved you, you should love each other. Your love for one another will prove to the world that you are my disciples" (John 13:34-35).

Sharing cements friendship.

The more you have FEARLESS CONVERSATIONS, the more you'll find that sharing two-way conversations is the cement that builds a solid foundation for friendships. If there's someone you want to become closer friends with, have a FEARLESS CONVERSATION with them and your relationship will inevitably go deeper.

Share your stories, and seek out the stories of others.

Listen.

In his book *The 7 Habits of Effective People,* Stephen Covey says, "Most people do not listen with the intent to understand; they listen with the intent to reply."[1]

Listening is a skill that every person on the planet can improve upon. If there's one thing you can practice and see immediate results, it's the art of listening. Hundreds, perhaps thousands, of books have been written about the importance of listening and how to become a better listener. (And let's be honest, how many of us have actually read any of those books?) It is indeed something that will not only improve your relationships, but it will give you amazing opportunities to show the love of Jesus to others.

When Chris was sharing his story with me about why he doesn't like Christians, he said he was weary of believers because they always seem to have a sales pitch. "When someone opens up," Chris said, "don't spout all your answers and tell them 'do this' and 'do that.' Don't give them your platitudes. Just be willing to listen."

Listening gives us the chance to cast our fears aside. Many Christians are afraid that they're being perceived as intolerant, close-minded, weak, unintelligent, or too political. Perhaps they're being perceived that way because they're always running off at the mouth about things. We can let those fears disappear when we begin to listen.

One time we watched a knowledgeable Bible-believing man dominate a Lifetree Café discussion about God and gays. No matter the question, he'd bark Scripture. He came off as harsh and unloving. He pushed people away—even the believers who probably agreed with him.

We wish we'd had the chance to "wonder" our way into his approach. We would have liked to have this kind of FEARLESS CONVERSATION with him one-on-one:

Me: I'm so glad you came to Lifetree Café today. From how you participate I can tell you spend lots of time in the Bible. I love Jesus and the Bible, too. *(Encourage and connect.)*

Me: I was wondering if I could talk with you about a couple things? *(Get permission.)*

If he says okay...

Me: I'm wondering what you hope happens with people when you quote Scripture?

If he answers...

Me: I wonder if you realize how you actually come off to others? What do you think?

If he replies...

Me: I wonder if you realize you quoting Scripture like you do (not listening), actually has the opposite effect?

We don't know how he'll respond. But this is our respectful, wondering conversation we have in our heads.

Are You Quick to Listen?

If you're not sure what kind of a listener you are, we've included a simple listening inventory. The following 20 statements pertain to how others might experience you as a listener. This nifty quiz is adapted from the book *Quick-to-Listen Leaders* by Dave Ping and Anne Clippard. Use the scale to rate your listening habits as you think your spouse, family members, friends, or co-workers who know you best would most likely describe you.

I, _____, am a person who:
(Your Name Here)

1. Gets impatient and annoyed when others express opinions that don't agree with mine.
   (1) practically never (2) very rarely (3) sometimes (4) frequently (5) almost always

2. Genuinely welcomes the opportunity to hear ideas, suggestions, and constructive feedback that could help my personal effectiveness.
   (1) almost always (2) frequently (3) sometimes (4) very rarely (5) practically never

3. Fidgets with objects, taps my hands or feet, or looks at the clock while others are speaking.
   (1) practically never (2) very rarely (3) sometimes (4) frequently (5) almost always

4. Takes plenty of time to consider what others are thinking and feeling before responding to what they say.
   (1) almost always (2) frequently (3) sometimes (4) very rarely (5) practically never

5. Mentally checks out and stops listening when people don't get to the point as quickly as I'd like them to.
   (1) practically never (2) very rarely (3) sometimes (4) frequently (5) almost always

6. Communicates that I'm interested by maintaining good eye contact and exercising open, friendly body language as others are talking.
   (1) almost always (2) frequently (3) sometimes (4) very rarely (5) practically never

7. Spends more time formulating my responses than actually listening.
   (1) practically never (2) very rarely (3) sometimes (4) frequently (5) almost always

8. Prepares to listen by removing anything that might distract me or create a barrier for those with whom I will be talking.
   (1) almost always (2) frequently (3) sometimes (4) very rarely (5) practically never

9. Changes the subject when a conversation begins to touch on emotional issues or when I don't like the direction it's going.
   (1) practically never (2) very rarely (3) sometimes (4) frequently (5) almost always

10. Accepts people first and then gets to know them rather than prejudging them based on how they look, talk, or what others have said about them.
    (1) almost always (2) frequently (3) sometimes (4) very rarely (5) practically never

11. Minimizes or discounts the opinions, experiences, and feelings of those with whom I disagree.
    (1) practically never (2) very rarely (3) sometimes (4) frequently (5) almost always

12. Stays engaged in conversations and relationships even when they become difficult or uncomfortable.
(1) almost always (2) frequently (3) sometimes (4) very rarely (5) practically never

13. Pontificates, lectures, or engages in long-winded monologues when it would be wiser to listen.
(1) practically never (2) very rarely (3) sometimes (4) frequently (5) almost always

14. Acts proactively in seeking honest input from those on whom my decisions or actions will have substantial impact.
(1) almost always (2) frequently (3) sometimes (4) very rarely (5) practically never

15. Uses the silent treatment and/or other forms of emotional blackmail to get my way or to get even with people who have displeased me.
(1) practically never (2) very rarely (3) sometimes (4) frequently (5) almost always

16. Tests my understanding of what others say by paraphrasing what they've said and repeating it back to them.
(1) almost always (2) frequently (3) sometimes (4) very rarely (5) practically never

17. Postpones necessary but unpleasant conversations or avoids them altogether.
(1) practically never (2) very rarely (3) sometimes (4) frequently (5) almost always

18. Initiates conversations with people who I believe might be upset with me to hear what is on their minds.
(1) almost always (2) frequently (3) sometimes (4) very rarely (5) practically never

19. Acts in ways that discourage people from approaching me and saying what's on their minds.
(1) practically never (2) very rarely (3) sometimes (4) frequently (5) almost always

20. Demonstrates a healthy sense of humor about my mistakes, foibles, and shortcomings.
(1) almost always (2) frequently (3) sometimes (4) very rarely (5) practically never

Overall Rating

Now, on a scale of 1 to 10, with 1 being "practically perfect" and 10 representing "very poor," rate your day-to-day performance in carrying out the biblical command to be "quick to listen, slow to speak, and slow to anger."

1   2   3   4   5   6   7   8   9   10

Scoring

As you took the inventory, you probably noticed that the odd-numbered questions focus on actions that get in the way of good listening and the even-numbered responses focus on helpful listening behaviors. To find your quick-to-listen score, add up all your responses. Compare your score to the scale below.

72-110—Slow. Like many Christians, you are much quicker to speak than listen. Practice listening more.

52-71—Steady. You're beginning to pull ahead of many others in your listening skills. With a little more work, you could be a quick-to-listen contender.

32-51—Skilled. You have the skills to be a quick-to-listen Christian. Practice them consistently, and you will be a life-changer.

21-31—Quick. You are a terrific listener (if you're not being overly optimistic in your self-assessment).[2]

Excerpt taken from *Quick-to-Listen Leaders*, published by Group Publishing, Inc., 1515 Cascade Ave., Loveland, CO 80538. group.com. Permission to photocopy this inventory granted for local church use. Copyright Equipping Ministries International, Inc.

> "Understand this, my dear brothers and sisters: **YOU MUST ALL BE QUICK TO LISTEN, SLOW TO SPEAK, AND SLOW TO GET ANGRY.**"
>
> —James 1:19

> "Let your conversation be gracious and attractive so that **YOU WILL HAVE THE RIGHT RESPONSE FOR EVERYONE.**"
>
> —Colossians 4:6

If you want respect, you must give respect.

Are atheists less than human? We watch a lot of Christians treat nonbelievers as though they're the spawn of Satan. In reality, they're just regular people with their fair share of questions and doubts. Are a few of them mean and aggressive? Sure. Are most of them open to a friendly conversation and sharing stories? Absolutely. We've seen it again and again through our Lifetree Café experience. In fact, some of our most "faithful" guests are nonbelievers (or not-quite-sure-believers).

Sadly, showing respect to others is one of the most difficult issues to overcome for many unloving Christians. They're staunch in their beliefs, convinced everyone else is wrong…period. They see no reason to respect those who don't think like they do.

Yet showing another person respect doesn't mean you have to accept or endorse their beliefs. It doesn't mean you're wavering in yours. It does mean that you show someone you recognize them as someone created and loved by God and that you care more about your relationship with them than proving yourself right.

Your respect is, in effect, your admission ticket to entering a relationship with someone. Without it, you'll never get past the doormat.

Fearless means connecting without fear.

Not long ago we talked with a man who may have had one of the most FEARLESS CONVERSATIONS in the history of FEARLESS CONVERSATIONS. His name is Daryl, and he told us about the time he got a chance to interview the Ku Klux Klan.

Daryl is black.

He spent his early years overseas with diplomat parents and came back to the U.S. in the '60s. Daryl was shocked and confused when he found himself being pelted with stones during a parade in which he marched as a Boy Scout. Befuddled, he asked his parents why people were throwing rocks at him. His parents told him about racism and how some people judge others by the color of their skin. Young Daryl couldn't believe it. How could someone hate him without even knowing him? That led him on a quest to talk with members of the KKK, the white supremacist group, so he could understand why they hated black people.

Daryl arranged to meet a KKK leader, a Grand Dragon, for a radio interview in a hotel room. The Grand Dragon was unaware that Daryl was black. Their initial meeting at the door was nothing short of awkward, but the two agreed to talk. They sat down, both surrounded by armed bodyguards. To ease the tension, Daryl offered a soft drink from the nearby ice bucket. Then Daryl pressed the tape recorder to "on." A sudden crashing sound made everyone jump. The bodyguards swooped in with their guns raised. Everyone looked around. Who made that sound? Who was ready to attack?

After a brief edgy moment, all eyes turned to the ice bucket. They realized the ice had shifted and created a crashing sound. Both parties realized their mistake, and everyone laughed. The ice was broken, literally and figuratively.

That FEARLESS CONVERSATION was just the beginning of many conversations that led to several KKK members turning in their robes to Daryl.

Astounding! By practicing the act of love through FEARLESS CONVERSATIONS, people were able to break down seemingly insurmountable barriers.

What are you afraid of? Surely that FEARLESS CONVERSATION you need to have isn't anywhere near as frightening as the one Daryl went through. Give your fear to God and take the leap in love.

95

Practice "backward gossip."

If you're going to speak of someone, speak kindly. This happens all the time at work for me (Joani). I remember bragging about a staff person to another co-worker. Much to my surprise, Becky—the person I was talking about—was right there within earshot. Wouldn't you rather get "caught" speaking kindly of someone than have them overhear you saying negative things about them? That can happen a lot when you practice what we call "backward gossip." When you speak of people to others, praise them.

Here's another positive outcome: When people realize that's how you treat others when they're not in your presence, they'll trust you to treat them the same. Your reputation as a genuine, loving Jesus-follower grows… and your faith becomes more and more magnetic.

Imagine both sides.

We have to remind ourselves all the time: There are always two sides (and usually more) to a story.

My (Thom's) journalism degree trained me in this most basic but often overlooked fact of life. Our weekly experiences in Lifetree Café have helped hone our skills as well. We'll never forget the episode called "Inside the Gun Debate." If you want to tackle a hot topic, this one is fiery-burning-red-blazing hot.

We interviewed two men, both with credible sides to their argument. Mike was a gun instructor who told the harrowing story of a walk he took with his little daughters when two Rottweilers chased them. Although Mike had his gun raised and was ready to shoot, the dogs' owners called off the growling animals just in time. He also talked about the night an intruder came into his hotel room ready to rob him. He pulled out his pistol, called the police, and was safe. Mike supports the right to bear arms.

On the other side of the issue was Dan, the father of one of the teens killed during the 1997 Columbine High School shooting. He shared his horrific experience of being called to the school and discovering that his son was murdered. He now wears his son's shoes as a symbol for the need to stop gun violence.

Two riveting stories. Two valid points of view from two real-life experiences. And the perfect topic for bringing people together to grow their relationships, right? Absolutely! By creating a safe environment for everyone to share their own stories and perspective, we were able to ask everyone to stop and consider the opposite side of their argument. Instead of a shouting match and unresolved anger, our time together resulted in deeper understanding and a civil dialogue. People left the room as friends with smiles on their faces.

We could use a whole lot more of that in our society today.

---

5 Uncomfortable Issues the Church Needs to Start Talking About
1. Addiction
2. Sexuality
3. Sincere doubt
4. Mental illness
5. Loneliness[3]

> God gave us two ears and
> one mouth for a reason.

Be present.

It's bad enough that church attendance has been declining steadily for years. Making matters far worse is the fact that the largest category of people who attend church services is a group we call PIBOs.

These folks are **Present In Body Only** (PIBO). They quietly walk into church, say little, look a bit detached, and leave quickly when the service concludes.

They may be counted as members of a church's flock, but their hearts, minds, and souls are not engaged by what's happening at church. They are among the legion of people who, according to George Barna, never experience God at church. They attend out of a sense of duty or to accompany a family member or simply out of habit. For PIBOs, the church worship experience—even at grandly produced services—is a spiritual yawn. The worship recipe (half upfront monologue and half sing-along) does not stir the PIBOs.

Many church leaders may not recognize these people as PIBOs—or even care that their hearts and minds are not in the room. Because PIBOs satisfy the measurement that leaders track, head count, they serve their purpose just as they are.

Don't be a PIBO.

It does nothing for your life, spiritually or otherwise, to be another warm body in the room. Instead, whether at church, at home, at work, or with friends and family, be present. Life's far too short not to be fully engaged in what you choose to do. God craves your full attention, as well as those who share a relationship with you. Your mental and emotional absence sends a clear message that you don't care, that you can't be bothered.

It's impossible for your faith to be magnetic when your mind is elsewhere. Wake up! There are roses that need to be smelled! Cookies that need to be shared! Love that needs to be given! Lives that need to be transformed!

Be open.

Many of us have a natural, reflective defense that makes us want to blurt out, "You're wrong!" whenever someone says something we disagree with. Part of having FEARLESS CONVERSATIONS is dropping your defenses. It may be hard to keep our mouths shut sometimes, but remember that if we want others to be open to us and our God, we need to be open to what they have to say, too. (It's part of that whole "do unto others" thing Jesus talked about.)

Kirsten Powers, a contributor to *USA Today,* columnist for *Newsweek* and *The Daily Beast*, and democratic commentator for Fox News, said being open was a key part of her path to finding a relationship with God. Before she believed in Jesus, she dated a Christian guy who asked her if she would be willing to keep an open mind about Christianity.

Kirsten said, "Well, of course. 'I'm very open-minded!' Even though I wasn't at all. I derided Christians as anti-intellectual bigots who were too weak to face the reality that there is no rhyme or reason to the world. I had found this man's church attendance an oddity to overlook, not a point in his favor.

"As he talked, I grew conflicted. On one hand, I was creeped out. On the other hand, I had enormous respect for him. He is smart, educated, and intellectually curious. I remember thinking, *What if this is true, and I'm not even willing to consider it?"*

Kirsten reluctantly went to church with him. She found herself fascinated by the pastor's sermon, which was intellectually rigorous and intriguing to her. Later she went to a Bible study, which she assumed was attended by "only weirdoes and zealots."

She said, "I don't remember what was said that day. All I know is that when I left, everything had changed. I'll never forget standing outside that apartment on the Upper East Side and saying to myself, 'It's true. It's completely true.' The world looked entirely different, like a veil had been lifted off it. I had not an iota of doubt. I was filled with incredible joy… Everywhere I turned, there [God] was. Slowly there was less fear and more joy. The Hound of Heaven had pursued me and caught me—whether I liked it or not."[4]

If we can hope for nonbelievers to keep an open mind about God and his love, surely we, too, can keep ourselves open to FEARLESS CONVERSATIONS that could lead people to Jesus. Being closed off doesn't make anyone's faith magnetic.

Some people we've talked to don't like the concept of being "open" with those who share different beliefs or who don't believe at all. When we dig deeper with them (asking "wondering" questions, of course), we learn that what they're really not open to is compromising their beliefs. That's not what we're advocating here. Being open to others simply means being open to conversation, open to listening, open to questions, and open to caring. Think of it as opening your heart to sharing God's love with others, no matter what.

Our friend Craig shared how using wondering questions helped him understand someone in a new way—and even helped a long-married couple grow closer. Here's his story:

"We have a Lifetree regular who, for a lack of a better word, is a little 'prickly.' He's an older gentleman and strong believer but a bit of a bull in a china shop when it comes to navigating grace-filled spiritual conversation.

"One day I joined a table where he and his wife were sitting with the hope of getting to know them a little better. During the course of the hour, the table talk conversation led to an opportunity to share our past experiences with being unfairly labeled. It was at that time that the wife shared how her husband is typically labeled as being very judgmental. I then asked the wondering question, 'I wonder how that makes you feel?' Her eyes welled up with tears and she began sharing the story of how it worries her greatly that her husband is often misunderstood, difficult to love, and quite lonely. She went on to say that about 10 years ago she had suffered a major stroke sending her into a coma for about a month. It was while she was in that hospital bed that she realized she had to survive for him. With tears streaming down his cheeks, he admitted to her that he never knew that story. He then shared with her that while she was unconscious in the hospital he had never left her bedside. He went on to say that he would hold his face close to hers and fervently pray that

God wouldn't take her. He said he knew that he couldn't go on living if he was to lose her.

"Imagine, a couple who had spent over 50 years together were learning something so dear and so intimate about each other for the first time at a place called Lifetree Café. That's the mystery and majesty of the Holy Spirit—and the power of a wondering question."

Refrain from incendiary words.

Your first response to this might be, "Well, of course! I would never use mean, hurtful words when I talk to nonbelievers." Name-calling and nastiness are the language of the ugly underworld of online trolls and divisive Christian extremists, right?

Not always. You'd be surprised at the list of "harmless" words we use every day that can turn people off. Overstated words like "always" and "never" send the message that you know best and leave no room for growth. Personalizing arguments (pointing fingers at people rather than sticking to the issues) always sparks a flame. Our churchy jargon (words and phrases like saved, justification, washed in the blood, or sinner) makes us sound pretentious at best, and at worst leaves others feeling mystified and excluded. Even seemingly benign teasing can cut deep and turn a friend away forever.

Refrain from "TRT," what our friend Jeanne Mayo refers to as "Typical Religious Talk." When we insist on speaking our own secret language, some of us Christians come off as uncaring, detached, and super spiritual, who talk more than we listen. And we can even come off as narcissists. "Those Christians are really into themselves. They only care about people who think and speak the way they do."

Like it or not, people are listening to every word we say.

A magnetic faith is one that attracts, not repels. So control your speech. Listen first. And don't forget how powerful your tongue can be for good or bad.

> "If you claim to be religious but don't control your tongue, **YOU ARE FOOLING YOURSELF, AND YOUR RELIGION IS WORTHLESS.**"
>
> —James 1:26

Fuel conversations with phrases such as...

How do you have a conversation with someone who believes differently? We've learned some no-fail phrases that draw out the best in people.

"I wonder..."

It's a genuine way of giving someone permission to speak their mind without being defensive or guarded.

"Could it be...?"

This is a great one in the midst of conflict. Instead of standing your ground with your opinion, simply add the phrase "Could it be...?" You'll open the door to conversation instead of shutting it. You're asking a question instead of making a declaration.

"Some people say..."

Referring to the opinions of others (or even your own in third person) helps to maintain common ground and avoids any personal conflict. It allows the other person to respond to an idea, rather than associating that idea with you or a specific person.

Ask "wondering" questions.

Instead of factoid questions, those who love with FEARLESS CONVERSATION engage in the art of "wondering." Our friend Doug Pollock, author of *God Space*, has perfected this skill. When someone says something that contradicts our Christian beliefs, we can ask, "I'm wondering what happened that led you to believe that?" Or "I'm wondering what you read that brought you to that conclusion?" By wondering, we can be respectfully, relationally curious as we delve into deeper understanding of someone.

Here's a sampling of some "wondering" questions. Take them for a test drive during your next conversation.

- Would you mind sharing with me the greatest piece of wisdom ever passed on to you?
- What do you like most about what you do? Least?
- If someone wanted to talk to you about God, how would you like to be approached?
- What images or words come to your mind when you hear the word *evangelism*?
- What is your dream job?
- Why do you think there are so many different religions?

- What conclusions have you come to concerning life after death?
- Have you ever been able to get a handle on what you think your purpose in life is?
- Do you consider yourself to be a Christian?
- Based on your understanding, how does someone become a Christian?
- As you've watched or read the news, what conclusions have you drawn about the nature of humanity?
- Have you ever had an experience in which you felt the presence of God?
- What causes you to struggle the most with the idea of God's existence?

The Power of Questions

In a University of North Carolina study, subjects were more receptive to advice from people who spoke tentatively ("Do you think you should…") than those who spoke powerfully ("You need to…").[5] This kind of "powerless communication" style helps convey vulnerability and respect for others' opinions.

Give the gift of "noticing."

We discovered a website called Q Place, and its goal is to facilitate safe and open discussions about God and faith. In their resource called *The Arts of Spiritual Conversations,* they outline nine everyday, relational practices that help Christians develop the ability to talk naturally about God with anyone. One of those practices is something called "noticing," and it's all about paying attention to what people are really saying and doing.

Our friend and co-worker Craig truly has the gift of noticing. It doesn't matter who he talks with, he's able to enter into amazing conversations. One day he shared with us a conversation he had with a newspaper reporter who was asking about an upcoming Lifetree Café episode, "Do Good Dogs Go to Heaven?" After the reporter finished the official interview, Craig practiced the gift of "noticing." He wondered and asked why the reporter was so interested in this story. It turns out that the Pittsburgh police had just lost one of their fellow "officers" a few days before by the name of Rocco—an 8-year-old German shepherd—and the city was grappling with the question of whether Rocco will be in heaven or not.

Maybe that might not matter much to you, but to that reporter and the people in the city, it mattered a lot. Incidentally, the "Do Good Dogs Go to Heaven" episode is one of the highest-ever attended Lifetree Cafés.

Pray.

Often.

Pray for the person who hurt you.

"You have heard the law that says, 'Love your neighbor and hate your enemy.' But I say, love your enemies! Pray for those who persecute you! In that way, you will be acting as true children of your Father in heaven" (Matthew 5:43-45).

Why does Jesus want us to pray for our enemies? Interestingly (and not surprisingly), science continues to discover Jesus' truths really work. Research published in the journal *Psychological Science* revealed that people who pray for a loved one who has hurt them harbor "fewer vengeful thoughts and emotions: They were more ready to forgive and move on… Prayer appears to shift attention from the self back to others, which allows the resentment to fade."[6]

Isn't that just like God?

Tell your own story, not platitudes.

As Chris and I (Joani) talked, he agreed that when Christians open up and share how God has worked in their lives or why they believe the way they do, he is more open. "Don't give platitudes or act like you have all the answers," Chris told me.

Bible-believing Christians who know the Word of God inside and out have a reputation for spouting Scripture verses that are disconnected from real life and real people's stories. People today are much more interested in how God worked authentically in your own life than Bible heroes. We're not saying Scripture is not powerful and relevant, but when it's used out of context from someone's own experience, it has little meaning for people. Yet when you can use the Bible in the context of how it's applied directly to someone's story (or your own story), it makes all the difference.

Here's an example from our friend Jeanne:

"This summer I spent a week in the Boundary Waters Canoe Area Wilderness with two other women, one of whom I'd never met before. These women, in my perspective, were very strong, self-confident, feminist women. They were both athletic and previously were physical education teachers and coaches. I, as you know, absolutely have no skill when it comes to anything athletic. To be honest, I was a bit scared to spend the week with them. And I must admit my feelings of being absolutely no good—those feelings I had in junior high school P.E. classes definitely came back alive and well.

"The new woman and I had a lot of conversations that went more in-depth than I thought we ever would have. I found myself talking about politics and religion, which we learned we were pretty much on the opposite ends of the spectrum. She commented on how much she appreciated hearing how I thought because it was different than what she expected from someone who votes as I do. She seemed to understand that I could take my religious beliefs and apply my values toward whom I voted for versus just voting for a person based on what he or she said was their religious background.

"By midweek I found myself one night in the tent having the courage to ask the question about her faith (she was Catholic), particularly about praying to saints. 'But you're praying to dead people,' I said. That led to a wonderful discussion of both women sharing the importance of the saints to them as intercessors. My friend mentioned that Jesus was too busy anyway to have time for everybody, so that's why the saints were there for them to pray to. I found myself exclaiming, 'No, I know Jesus is always there for you!'"

Jeanne built her relationship with these women on personal stories, and when those personal experiences led to it, Jeanne felt an opening to share specifics about her faith.

It's okay to share your own experiences and struggles. Once one person opens up, the other will reciprocate.

Admit you have questions.

You've probably heard hard questions like these: Why do there seem to be contradictions in the Bible? Why are there so many denominations and different interpretations of the Bible? How can people claim to be Christian but not act like it? How come the biblical account of creation doesn't sound scientifically possible?

If we're honest, Christians have to admit that we don't have all the answers. Some questions can't be answered. That's where faith comes in. When we grow a meaningful relationship with God through our faith, we accept that there are some things we just don't understand. We choose to trust God that he knows what he's doing.

We talk to a lot of pastors on a regular basis, and one thing we've heard from many of them is that they feel like they can never say "I don't know."

In their eyes, it's forbidden for pastors and other church leaders not to have the answers. That's unfortunate.

One of the reasons some people are turned off by Christians is because they consider Christians to be arrogant in their belief that they have *the* answer for everything. But when we admit that we, too, have some unanswered questions, it opens the door to growing your relationships with those who wonder. Sometimes it's okay to say, "I don't know. Let's see if we can find out together." Hard questions give us a wonderful opportunity to grapple together and even lead you and your friends to seek out the Bible and other believers for answers.

Invite others to meet your friend Jesus.

When we see faith as a relationship, we understand that our Christian faith isn't about being right or debating subjects. It's about truly loving others and wanting them to meet your friend Jesus.

Imagine your best friends. If you're like us, you revel in introducing your best friends to each other. We remember Matt and Shawna's wedding. Not only were we ecstatic about their marriage, but we were excited to share the occasion and introduce our great friends to our other great friends. It was so much fun to bring people together and say, "You just have to meet our friend, Rolf! Jeanne! Nancy! Bruce! My mom!"

That's just like introducing others to Jesus. When the time is right, it's perfectly appropriate to share why Jesus has been such a special friend to you and how much he means to you.

Compare that approach to this one: "You're going to hell if you don't believe in Jesus." So many people think that's what Christians care about. Instead, God wants us to create an atmosphere of love so he can do his part and work in people's lives…in his own time.

Paula is a vivacious young woman who grew up in a Christian home with a father who taught theology at a Christian university. She told us that she felt like she always had to be perfect. Of course, that's impossible. It crushed her. So she rebelled and left her family and her faith for 25 years. She was the picture of the prodigal son in Luke chapter 11, only she was the "prodigal daughter." Her parents thought she had abandoned them… and God. But God hadn't left Paula. Miraculously, and with God's timing, she returned to her roots. Now she and her dad work together to help heal other ministers who have prodigal kids. They work at healing relationships with families—and God.

Be interested in others.

You've heard it said that to be interesting you must be interested. That may be the best "rule" of conversation. Be curious. Really care about what the other person is saying.

Our friend and co-worker Rick says you should always ask "one more" question. It takes practice, and it can be exhausting to begin with. And there's an art to it. You want to be interested...but not probing. You want to be engaged...but not invasive. You need to feel when the other person doesn't want to go there.

Thom teases me (Joani) because I end up in conversations with strangers all the time, and they often tell me things they say they haven't told anyone else. I credit it to the fact that I truly am interested in them—I love people! I love their stories!—and they sense that right away. It's one of those basic needs we talked about in Chapter 1. People want to be seen and known.

Be willing to be vulnerable.

To love someone, we must give, too. We're amazed at the depth of conversation we get to when we share our weaknesses. When I (Thom) have opened up to the staff at Group about company difficulties or mistakes we've made, people have been forgiving. When I (Joani) share my health issues or personal fears and failures, people lean in.

Too often we wrongly think that if we let others know we don't have it all together, they'll think less of us somehow. But, in fact, they'll think more of us.

We recommend watching Brené Brown's TED talk on vulnerability. You can find it online at ted.com/talks/brene_brown_on_vulnerability. We think you'll find it inspiring and thought provoking.

Create a safe climate.

Tell your friends that you welcome their thoughts and their doubts. Hold onto the belief that we can have differing viewpoints while maintaining respect and love for one another.

We live in an age of sharp political division and rude talk-show brawls. Outrage is running rampant in every corner of our society. But loving others means we can exchange opinions without exchanging blows. Disagreements are our opportunity to produce the fruit of the Spirit. Christians should be the ones showing love, joy, peace, patience, kindness, goodness, faithfulness, gentleness, and self-control in conversations of every kind.

My (Thom's) family lives that out. When we gather around the family table for special occasions, the conversations are robust. Family members let their differing political and religious beliefs fly. It doesn't mean people don't disagree—we do—but we still show love and respect. We leave the table with our smiles and hearts intact. We know it's a safe place of unconditional love.

Sadly, there are some Christians who just can't bring themselves into this safe place. Bert shared his comments about his experience with Christians who just can't get past the disagreements: "The challenge is that the more controversial [fearless] the conversation becomes, the greater the possibility that someone won't like an expressed opinion, or they may not like the fact that competing ideas are offered and discussed energetically. [At church] we've had people leave in the middle of an hour and tell the pastor later it was a horrible experience for them. They apparently felt that people who were in disagreement couldn't possibly love each other—or they simply couldn't tolerate listening to ideas with which they disagreed. For some, the idea that FEARLESS CONVERSATION can be done in love seems impossible to consider. But for those who are up to it, we have a good time."

We always have a good time! In our experience through Lifetree Café and its long list of controversial topics, we've seen perhaps 99 percent of the participants find a way to disagree with love and respect. We know it's not only possible, but absolutely necessary.

Take time.

"You must take the time over a cup of coffee. Or a thousand cups of coffee," our friend Jeanne likes to say. Or over wine or beer or meals, our other friends remind us. Invest in relationships. Be the one someone can count on, because you've done the heavy lifting of spending time together. We can't begin to tell you the friends that God has blessed us with and who we have enjoyed over the many, many years. Yes, we've gone through life over the miles and years with friends. Marriages, divorces, births, deaths, illnesses, cancer, addictions, job changes, job losses, and miracles. They all take time, and they all play a role through this ongoing and unpredictable journey called life.

Take time, and let God take his.

107

Ask the unexpected question.

This gem comes from Sasha Vyaska, an oncologist who deals with death every day. Her direct nature probably comes from not having the luxury of time in her relationships with breast cancer patients. She told us about a time she was waiting at an elevator in the hospital. She noticed a man and unexpectedly asked him how he was doing. She wasn't sure what prompted her to ask, but she found out he was getting his wife because she'd just given birth to a stillborn baby, and he was hurting. After 20 minutes and a few elevator doors opening and closing, she had experienced an act of love through FEARLESS CONVERSATION.

Asking "how are you?" and not settling for a "fine" response would be asking the unexpected question. To really care and want to know carves a path to a deeper friendship.

Seek to understand.

When practicing FEARLESS CONVERSATION, Christians need to try to grasp why someone thinks, feels, or responds a certain way. This skill is not easy. Because we view the world through our own lens of experiences, it requires thinking of others before ourselves—a loving, Jesus-style trait.

When seeking to understand others, we can deal with real-life issues in a way that keeps relationships intact. During a Lifetree Café episode called "God and Gays," participants practiced seeking to understand. We received these comments from Lifetrees around the country:

"Difficult subject handled very well."

"Very good conversation and made me think. It gave me a desire to continue to search what God says about the issue."

"Very interesting, yet touchy subject. This was discussed without bashing others. Thank you!"

It *is* possible to seek understanding without hitting people over the head with our Bibles or establishing walls with our beliefs. Seeking to understand shows others that we seek to love them.

Choose to remember.

Our friend Justin has trained himself to excel in one of the best skills you can have when it comes to showing people you care about them: He remembers. One time we watched him remember a parking lot attendant's birthday—just a tiny sample of what Justin does with everyone he meets. It's a remarkable talent...and you can do it too. (More about Justin's story in the next chapter.)

Jot down details. Use a notebook or your smartphone contact list to add details about special dates, kids' and spouses' names, favorite restaurants, quirky funny things. Find a way that works for you, and try it out with a small number of people you'd like to build a relationship with, as well as with a few who might least expect it.

We have a couple friend, Bob and Karen, whom we enjoy having dinner with at one of our favorite restaurants in town. One evening when the waitress brought back our check with credit cards, she sincerely said, "Thank you, Mr. Flier." *Who's Mr. Flier?* we wondered. After she left, we all looked at each other and burst into laughter. She had misread Bob's credit card that noted he was a "frequent flier." So now in the "choose to remember" region of my brain, I (Joani) have jotted that memory in my contact list. It's a quirky detail. But a meaningful, fun memory touchpoint whenever we see Bob and Karen.

Trust the Holy Spirit.

This may be the greatest missing ingredient in our Christian lives today. We like to be the ones in control. We hold onto our lives, relationships, and faith like we're gripping white knuckled to our steering wheels. We need to relax. Let go of our tight grip. And trust the Holy Spirit. We worry down to the minutest detail, leaving no room for God to actually work. The only problem is we do all the talking and figure God may be only speaking through us—and no one else.

When we trust the Spirit to produce fruit from our FEARLESS CONVERSATIONS, we have nothing to be afraid of. It's God's Spirit that makes it possible for our conversations to be fearless.

Let Scripture speak for itself.

Inject relevant Scripture into your discussions, not as a proof text but as a resource and light. Resist the temptation to contort the Scripture into saying something more than it actually says. Let others explore how the Scripture may apply to their lives. And if different passages provide different perspectives, encourage grappling together with those contrasting perspectives.

Say thank you and affirm others.

Encouraging others, thanking people, and sincerely complimenting people never gets old. Years ago we led a workshop on the keys to a successful youth group meeting. We said that affirmation was the one secret ingredient that would keep kids coming back. They're usually not even aware that it's happening, but affirmation leaves them with a positive taste in their mouth and eager for more.

The most profound example of affirmation and encouragement happens every summer at our Group Mission Trips. More than 25,000 teens and their adult leaders get "care cards" in a manila envelope with their name on it. Throughout the week, campers are challenged to write a care card for each person in their crew every day. The care card must be positive and uplifting (no put-downs allowed). By the end of the week, every envelope is stuffed with affirmation that shows each person how God worked through them that week. Since the inception of Group Workcamps (1977), care cards remain one of the favorite secret ingredients to the Group Mission Trips experience. Years later we hear from people who have kept their care cards and are still affirmed by them today. It never gets old to get a dose of encouragement. We firmly believe that's how God works.

The best part is it works with any age. Most people may not be able to articulate what it was about their time together, but it feels good when someone says thank you. At Lifetree Café we say, "Thank you for sharing," "Thank you for taking the risk," "Thank you for civil conversation." It's a way that we demonstrate Jesus' love. We believe thanking others in FEARLESS CONVERSATIONS is what makes our faith magnetic. It's like Jesus. People were drawn to his love.

Use direct communication.

This idea is not new. In fact, it's biblical. But few people actually practice it.

It's one of the cornerstones for our success in our business. Each month, we meet with new Group staff to welcome them to our company. We listen to everyone introduce themselves, find out about their families, hobbies, and interests. Plus we invite them to share "How in the world did you get to Group?" Because we've done this for years, we anticipate miraculous stories of God's divine intervention and guidance. After we share those stories, we congratulate them for being part of an exemplary team that God has pulled together. After all the storytelling, we remind them of a secret to success here at Group. Everyone leans in. Here it comes. What will the boss say are the secrets to success in my job?

With everyone's attention, I (Thom) lean in and say, "Direct communication." Inevitably, a few eyebrows raise. We know they're thinking it must be something more profound. But we believe direct communication is one of the secrets of great relationships. Go to the person who can do something about whatever it is you need. It's so simple.

110

This one simple, straightforward, biblical mandate can prevent all kinds of problems. For example, we say if your co-worker is snapping their gum and it drives you up your cubicle wall, tactfully say, "You might not realize it, but when you snap your gum, I can hear it, and it makes me lose my concentration." Imagine how much quicker that issue is resolved than griping to other co-workers how inconsiderate and rude your cubemate is.

> Jesus says,
> "If another believer sins against you, go privately and point out the offense. If the other person listens and confesses it, you have won that person back. **BUT IF YOU ARE UNSUCCESSFUL, TAKE ONE OR TWO OTHERS WITH YOU AND GO BACK AGAIN, SO THAT EVERYTHING YOU SAY MAY BE CONFIRMED BY TWO OR THREE WITNESSES.**"
>
> —Matthew 18:15-16

It gets tricky sometimes. Imagine your boss has given you too much to do, and there's no way you will get it done by the end of the week. What to do? Go to your leader (the one who can do something about it) and say, "Looking at all these projects, I realize I won't be able to get everything done." Then propose a solution: "Are the deadlines firm? Would next week be okay? Or if I prioritize this project instead, I could get it done. Or do we need to bring in extra help?" Leaders value staff who are tactfully direct and provide suggestions for solutions. Too many people talk to others who can't do anything about a situation, complain, or use body language (sigh, roll eyes, cross arms) in an effort to communicate a message that does nothing but get lost and make matters worse.

Don't be afraid. Don't gossip. Go have that conversation with the person who can do something about it.

Treat online conversations as though they were face to face.

The Web, blogs, Facebook, Twitter, and more have allowed for thoughtless, hurtful comments to be hurled about. Before you write anything, imagine that person being in front of you. Would you say that to a friend? Let's bring civility to the Web.

Ask permission.

Any time you face a tough conversation, ask permission: "If it's okay with you…" or "Would you be open to me sharing…."

We've discovered through Lifetree Café that when we pray, we always ask first if it's okay: "If it's alright with you, I'd like to say a prayer." In all the years of doing Lifetree Cafés with Christians, atheists, pagans, witches, Muslims, you name it, no one has said no. No one has complained.

It's the same in a caring relationship. We're moved by someone who asks if he or she could pray for us. We're drawn to those who respect us, so when you say, "I really care about you, and I'm wondering if I could share with you…or what's troubling me is…or what I seeing happening in your life is…or what I've heard is going on with you is…." When we care enough to ask the other person if it's okay, chances are they will see our love and concern shine through.

Have you lost your fear yet?

We could go on and on with tips and advice on how to have FEARLESS CONVERSATIONS. Of the 4 ACTS OF LOVE, it may be the one that has the most profound, practical implications for building relationships based on faith. It may also be the most obvious way to make your faith magnetic with everyone you know.

But the next act of love, GENUINE HUMILITY, can be just as powerful and perhaps the most elusive for many people. Let's explore how loving others through GENUINE HUMILITY can make your faith in Jesus truly irresistible.

Endnotes

1. Stephen R. Covey, *The 7 Habits of Highly Effective People: Powerful Lessons in Personal Change* (New York, NY: Simon & Schuster, 1989), 251.

2. Dave Ping and Anne Clippard, *Quick-to Listen Leaders: Where Life-Changing Ministry Begins* (Loveland, CO: Group Publishing, 2005), 23-25.

3. Zach Perkins, "5 Uncomfortable Issues the Church Needs to Start Talking About," RELEVANT Magazine, December 9, 2013, http://www.relevantmagazine.com/god/church/5-uncomfortable-issues-church-needs-start-talking-about.

4. Kirsten Powers, "Fox News' Highly Reluctant Jesus Follower" Christianity Today, October 22, 2013, http://www.christianitytoday.com/ct/2013/november/fox-news-highly-reluctant-jesus-follower-kirsten-powers.html.

5. Allison Fragale, "The power of powerless speech: The effects of speech style and task interdependence on status conferral," Department of Organizational Behavior and Strategy, Kenan-Flagler Business School, University of North Carolina, Chapel Hill, NC, March 15, 2005.

6. Association for Psychological Science, "Prayer increases forgiveness, study shows," ScienceDaily, February 1, 2010, http://www.sciencedaily.com/releases/2010/01/100127134607.htm.

6 GENUINE HUMILITY

Have you ever been blown away by someone's **GENUINE HUMILITY?**

We have a friend, Justin Mayo, who lives in Los Angeles and spends much of his time in big cities around the world. He's a likeable, genuine young guy with an unusual goal in life: to offer unconditional love to young creative and influential people around the world. He's got big dreams to go along with his big heart.

You probably haven't heard of Justin, but you've definitely heard of many of his friends. He runs in the "beautiful people" crowd. Movie stars, philanthropists, musicians, artists, princes, politicians, and all sorts of other famous people. We don't know how, but he's been invited to the White House, and he once lunged to hug the president (to the angst of the secret service guys!) just because the president looked like he needed a hug.

Justin cares about each one of those people as a person, not just for their fame or talents. He's the kind of person you'd call a true friend. We know Justin, and we can tell you he's the real deal.

The names on his speed dial may amaze you, but what's far more amazing is how Justin's dream and heart reaches the "little" people too. His organization, Red Eye, exists to match the "greatest of these" with the "least of these." He arranges Mother's Day makeovers on Skid Row. He hosted his own birthday party for kids in the inner city. He connects talented professionals with kids in the projects to act as mentors every Saturday. He throws cool "senior proms" for seniors in a Hollywood retirement home. That's what Justin does—he brings unlikely people together to show love through RADICAL HOSPITALITY…and he does it with GENUINE HUMILITY.

We've been so intrigued with Justin's out-of-the-ordinary approach that we've videotaped some of his events and interviewed the special people who've attended. You can't help welling up with tears as you watch some of Hollywood's best makeup artists put lipstick and eye shadow on low-income moms, helping them feel beautiful for the first time in their lives. There's an inexpressible joy in watching glamorous young adults throw a rollicking prom, complete with a DJ, red carpet, mirror ball, decorations, snacks, and punch, and then crowning the prom king and queen from the cast of lonely old folks who live in that retirement community. It's real love, and it's at full volume for everyone to hear.

After one of our visits, Justin insisted he take us to the SoHo House for dinner. Little did we know we were about to encounter the Hollywood scene. We drove there in our cheap compact rental car. It looked rather out of place among the fancy cars with names you only ever see on TV. Wide-eyed, we checked in with the hostess. Reservations and a club membership are required. The hostess kindly told us we could climb the elegant marble staircase beneath the glittering chandelier and wait for Justin in the garden room—a magical rooftop restaurant glistening with trees all lit up with twinkling lights. It was enchanting! Our jaws hung open like some kind of backwater tourists, so Thom whipped out his smartphone to snap a picture. Within seconds, bodyguards surrounded us. "Erase those photos! No photos allowed!" Gulp. We understand that famous people do tire of pictures all the time. Reprimand received. Evidence erased.

Soon Justin rescued us. He introduced us to two new friends, and we enjoyed a great dinner and conversation about what it's like to be a Jesus-follower in Tinseltown. Meanwhile, we caught a glimpse of Cher at the table behind us. (She still looks really good, by the way!) There were other stars twinkling around us, but by now we knew the rules. Justin, however, seems to play by his own rules. We smiled in amazement as he introduced us to movers and shakers in this exclusive club…as well as the wait staff, who appeared to be just as good of friends with Justin as the big wigs.

As we returned to our car, Justin walked up to the parking garage attendant, whom Justin called by name.

"Wasn't it your birthday yesterday?" Justin asked.

"Aw, Justin, how'd you remember that?" the attendant replied with a big smile on her face.

Above all else, that was the moment that was seared in our memories.

We realize one of the reasons we love being with Justin is that he overflows GENUINE HUMILITY. He willingly and joyfully lives out the love of Jesus to everyone—truly everyone—he knows. No matter how great or small the personal encounter, he's got a smile, a hug, and a kind word.

Isn't that what makes Jesus so magnetic? Jesus embraces all of us with unconditional love, no matter our status, our past, our whatever. Jesus himself offers us GENUINE HUMILITY.

What Is **GENUINE HUMILITY?**

It's an odd thing that humility is a concept that eludes so many Christians. The Bible talks a lot about the importance of humility, and yet it seems so few Christians actually practice it. In the first chapter we talked about one of the top reasons people don't like to be around Christians. Number two on the list: hypocrisy. It's not just about saying one thing and doing another. People call Christians hypocrites because they act as though they have all the right answers. Christians have a reputation for pointing their fingers at everyone else, as if their own lives are somehow free from flaws and shortcomings. Believers have a habit of insisting that they're right, but to everyone else, that's the height of arrogance. That's the opposite of GENUINE HUMILITY.

What is *not* GENUINE HUMILITY?

- Humility is not self-deprecation.
- Humility is not being insecure in who you are.
- Humility is not being defined by your faults, your lack of abilities, your quirks, your oddities, and your flaws.
- Humility is not belittling yourself in hopes of receiving little nuggets of hollow praise.
- Humility is not an act of comparing yourself to others and deciding you're something less. You'll always find someone who's better than you or worse than you. But you're focusing on the wrong things when it comes to measuring your worth.
- Humility is not saying "I'm so humbled" when you win first place.
- Humility is not judging others and then claiming that "I'm just the Lord's humble servant doing the Lord's work."

We love this quote, attributed to C.S. Lewis: "True humility is not thinking less of yourself; it is thinking of yourself less." That's it in a nutshell, but we'll spend the rest of this chapter unpacking the depth and practical implications of what that really means.

GENUINE HUMILITY *is*:

- Being radically relational. That means meeting people on an equal plane, knowing we're all at different places on the spiritual spectrum. It means caring about your relationship with others, no matter where they're at in their faith journey—even if they've wandered off the path altogether.

- Being open to learning from others with different beliefs. No matter who you are or how much you've studied the Bible, we're pretty sure you're not right about everything. (And neither are we!) We consider ourselves lifelong learners.

- Being open to learning from people of different ages. All of us can learn from children. All of us can learn from our elders. We're simultaneously *all* teachers. *All* learners. No matter which stage of life we're in, we all have life experiences and perspectives that can provide insight to others.

- Admitting mistakes. We, as the body of Christ, have our flaws, but that's what being the church is all about. None of us is perfect, and we all need God's hand in our lives. So when people say, "Christians are a bunch of hypocrites," we need to admit that, yes, we too are indeed flawed.

> "Healthy people don't need a doctor—**SICK PEOPLE DO.**"
>
> —Jesus, Luke 5:31

- Free from insider language. Being humble means setting aside everything that excludes others, and that includes the words we use. Christians speak a lingo that few outsiders understand, which perpetuates an "us and them" mentality rather than a "we're all in this together" approach.

- Communicating directly. If there's one thing we've learned about working with people over the years, it's that open, clear, and straightforward communication always—*always*—makes for a healthier and happier home, family, friends, workplace, and church. Direct communication shows a pure willingness not to place yourself above others and make sure everyone's plugged in.

This chapter will help you understand what GENUINE HUMILITY looks like in everyday life. We'll give you examples, tell you stories, and give you loads of tips on how to be genuinely humble as a Christian. When people see your GENUINE HUMILITY in action, they can't help but be magnetized by your loving faith.

> "Make it your goal to live a quiet life, minding your own business and working with your hands, just as we instructed you before. **THEN PEOPLE WHO ARE NOT CHRISTIANS WILL RESPECT THE WAY YOU LIVE, AND YOU WILL NOT NEED TO DEPEND ON OTHERS."**
> —1 Thessalonians 4:11-12

A BIBLICAL Definition

Here's the biblical explanation of Jesus' GENUINE HUMILITY. Use these words from Scripture as a prayer for following Jesus' example:

"Though he was God, he did not think of equality with God as something to cling to. Instead, he gave up his divine privileges; he took the humble position of a slave and was born as a human being. When he appeared in human form, he humbled himself in obedience to God and died a criminal's death on a cross.

119

"Therefore, God elevated him to the place of highest honor and gave him the name above all names, that at the name of Jesus every knee should bow, in heaven and on earth and under the earth, and every tongue confess that Jesus Christ is Lord, to the glory of God the Father" (Philippians 2:6-11).

BYE-BYE Comfort Zone

While Justin may seem completely at ease with showing love to every person he meets, we find ourselves having to step out of our comfort zones on a regular basis. Our experiment with Lifetree Café has been no exception. It's a weekly exercise in GENUINE HUMILITY. Over the past five years we've interviewed and had spiritual conversations with every imaginable kind of person—religious experts, politicians, UFO abductees, ghost hunters, cancer survivors, pet psychics, famous authors, counselors, tragedy survivors, humanitarians, Bible scholars, vampire fanatics, researchers, scientists, and scores of regular people on this journey called life.

Regularly rubbing shoulders with people who are different from us offers amazing opportunities to practice Jesus-style humility.

One great example of this was the day we met Rose Elizabeth.

We traveled to the D.C. area to join our friend Doug, who'd arranged an interview with the father of one of his co-workers. The father had just revealed that he had become…she. We knew transgenderism would be a fascinating story to discuss at Lifetree Café.

I (Joani) still remember knocking on the door of a modest home in a D.C. suburb. I'd never had any connections to anyone claiming to be transgender. I didn't know what to expect, and I had butterflies in my stomach. Honestly, the whole concept rattled my sensibilities. I had to shake my prejudices and pray for God to grant me a giant dose of acceptance. I had no idea what to expect, but I prayed for a humble and loving heart.

The door opened. We were warmly greeted by a smiling, husky-voiced person wearing a perfect page-boy wig. Rose Elizabeth made us feel at home as we set up the camera and settled in for the interview. For the next few hours, Rose Elizabeth revealed his/her life-long struggle with feeling like a woman trapped in a man's body.

Now, I don't know how stuff like this happens in God's plan, but I do know God loves Rose Elizabeth. We had to suspend our "we're better than you" attitudes. We met Rose Elizabeth on common ground as people searching for peace, love, and God's wisdom.

This was a unique encounter where God truly reached in. I believe God wanted us to demonstrate acceptance, love, understanding, curiosity, respect, and GENUINE HUMILITY. God used Rose Elizabeth to teach us all those things. And we're thankful for that. God also taught us it's not always easy and natural to be a servant and not lord yourself over someone else.

The Lifetree Café episode "When He Becomes a She" gave communities everywhere a chance to reach a group of people who are often misunderstood, outcast, and longing for acceptance. What transpired during those hours would fill another book! God showed up as people reached out in GENUINE HUMILITY to love others.

Lifestyle differences aren't the only things that call us to show GENUINE HUMILITY. Maybe some of the hardest for us as Christians are differences in beliefs. We've come face to face with Muslims, Mormons, conspiracy theorists, UFOlogists, ghost hunters, psychics, and many more people who don't view the world through the same lenses we do.

It's rare for Christians today to invite people with differing beliefs to grapple together instead of pushing to prove each other wrong. We recently experienced a Lifetree episode called "Mormons: Christian? Cult? What Do They Really Believe?" We were taken aback by a comment from one of the Mormons in attendance: "This was a surprise. Thank you for the respectful conversation. We're usually ambushed."

What does that say about Christians' reputation?

What's So Compelling About **GENUINE HUMILITY?**

It requires us to "do unto others as we would have them do unto us." Would you want to be invited to someone's home only to have the host tell you everything you think and do is wrong? We all have flaws and misdirected beliefs. We're all sinners. But most of us don't respond well when we are impugned rather than loved.

> "For everyone has sinned; **WE ALL FALL SHORT OF GOD'S GLORIOUS STANDARD.**"
>
> —Romans 3:23

It can be challenging to relinquish control and refrain from setting ourselves up as experts, especially if we've poured a lifetime into theological training or years of Bible studies and discipleship courses. All those things are good, but no one likes a know-it-all. Plus, setting ourselves up as Bible gurus can produce the ugly side effects of pride and ego, which have become poison in the church and solidified our reputation as hypocrites.

To exhibit GENUINE HUMILITY, we must admit "we're *all* in this together." As humans, we're all on this journey of life. We must admit we don't have all the answers. When we show we're as eager and open to grow as those who don't have a relationship with Jesus, we invite others on this exciting God-journey. By asking questions we become more like Jesus, the Master Asker. Even though Jesus is God, he asked loads of questions and valued grappling and discovery, always sure of his relationship with God the Father.

Remember, we live in an age of immediate access to abundant information. People aren't hungering for more information. They crave authentic, humble, Jesus-centered relationships.

JESUS-STYLE
Genuine Humility

Imagine having dinner with your friends and Jesus. You're intrigued and wonder a lot about the One who claims to be God. You watch Jesus get up from the table, take off his robe, wrap a towel around his waist, and pour water into a basin. What is he up to? It's awkward, weird, mysterious, and even a bit off-putting. He moves from one person to the next washing their feet and gently drying them with his towel. Gross. Not surprisingly, Peter protests. Jesus responds, "You don't understand now what I am doing, but someday you will" (John 13:7).

Do any of us really understand the magnitude of Jesus' actions? He's God, for Pete's sake! He shouldn't have to literally stoop so low. Yet Jesus does. In every way, in everything he did, he stooped so low as to serve us so we could be with him forever.

The night of the foot washing, Jesus also said, "Do you understand what I was doing? You call me 'Teacher' and 'Lord,' and you are right because that's what I am. And since I, your Lord and Teacher, have washed your feet, you ought to wash each other's feet. I have given you an example to follow. Do as I have done to you. I tell you the truth, slaves are not greater than their master. Nor is the messenger more important than the one who sends the message. Now that you know these things, God will bless you for doing them" (John 13:12-17).

So much transpired that night. In the midst of the events before Jesus' brutal death, he reminded his friends that their ultimate purpose was to be like him: "So now I am giving you a new commandment: Love each other. Just as I have loved you, you should love each other. Your love for one another will prove to the world that you are my disciples" (John 13:34-35).

GENUINE HUMILITY as Jesus lived it was wrapped in love and serving others. If the God of the universe could come to earth as a tiny, helpless baby who grew up and gave away his life for us, is it too much to ask that we strive to give our lives away in love? That we never think of ourselves as better than others?

Imagine Jesus saying, "We're all in this together." We all struggle. We all have questions. None of us has it all together. GENUINE HUMILITY admits that all of us are going through life together, and we all need God's love to get us through it.

No better passage sums up Jesus' example of
GENUINE HUMILITY than Philippians 2:1-11.
Use this Scripture passage to rate your level of
GENUINE HUMILITY. How's your score?

IS THERE ANY ENCOURAGEMENT FROM BELONGING TO CHRIST?

Hardly Ever ⟵————————————————⟶ Most of the Time

ANY COMFORT FROM HIS LOVE?

Hardly Ever ⟵————————————————⟶ Most of the Time

ANY FELLOWSHIP TOGETHER IN THE SPIRIT?

Hardly Ever ⟵————————————————⟶ Most of the Time

IS YOUR HEART TENDER AND COMPASSIONATE?

Hardly Ever ⟵————————————————⟶ Most of the Time

Then make Jesus truly happy by...

agreeing wholeheartedly with each other,
loving one another,
working together with one mind and purpose.
Don't be selfish;
don't try to impress others.
Be humble, thinking of others better than yourself.
Don't look out only for your own interests,
But take an interest in others, too.
You must have the same attitude that Christ Jesus had.

YOUR PRESENCE
Is Required

In the last chapter we talked about the need to be present and how so many Christians have become PIBOs (Present In Body Only) in their faith. These are the believers who may be sitting in church, but their hearts and minds are off somewhere else—maybe thinking of the football game, their grocery list, what they might have for lunch—anything other than the sermon. (Which, by the way, is an issue church leaders need to resolve. Sermons have very little to do with growing anyone's faith. You can read more about that in our previous book, *Why Nobody Wants to Go to Church Anymore.*)

PIBOs aren't just in churches. They're in restaurants, on the couch, and in the car. They're glued to their cellphones. Maybe they're with us, but they're not really *with* us. If you're honest, you have probably had some PIBO moments in your own life.

When you're in PIBO mode, you aren't showing GENUINE HUMILITY. Without speaking a single word, you're telling everyone around you that they're not important to you. You're saying, "I'm not here for you. I probably wouldn't even notice if you weren't here." Harsh? Yes. But PIBOs have zero magnetic faith.

124

When we show GENUINE HUMILITY, we're authentically present for those we're with. We're literally face to face, eye to eye, proving with our body language that we're fully engaged. That, unfortunately, is a rare gift. Yet what a remarkable opportunity for Christians to show love.

We experience GENUINE HUMILITY every week with new friends at Lifetree Café. We sit at small round tables of four, practically forcing everyone to be present and look each other in the eye. It's intimate, it's real, and it gives people a chance to practice that kind of authentic act of love.

Offering the gift of our presence is something we can give freely, every day, with anyone we connect with. We don't even have to say anything! Our full attention and our listening ears are exactly what people need when they're experiencing a hardship. We may never know the right words to say, and that's okay. Don't say anything. Just be present. GENUINE HUMILITY means it's not about you; it's about the ones you love.

We'll never forget when I (Thom) went to the funeral of our hairdresser's son who died an untimely death. I didn't say anything. I was simply present. And that meant a lot to our friend. (Although I did have to smile when our friend said her mother thought I was the undertaker!)

Another practical way to be present (a non-PIBO) is to look at people when you speak with them. We know from experience how awkward it is to be at a party and the person you're talking to keeps glancing away, perhaps on the lookout for someone more important or exciting than you. You surprise people when you're fully present. They can truly feel the love you're showing them through your GENUINE HUMILITY.

> "Then the name of our Lord Jesus will be honored because of the way you live, and you will be honored along with him. **THIS IS ALL MADE POSSIBLE BECAUSE OF THE GRACE OF OUR GOD AND LORD, JESUS CHRIST.**"
>
> —2 Thessalonians 1:12

A Travel Parable From
New Guinea and Vanuatu

GENUINE HUMILITY goes both ways. I (Joani) have had to humble myself on our travels because I'm not physically able to balance very well or walk distances. Because I have multiple sclerosis, it impedes my physical abilities. (But I'm not letting that stop me—it just slows me down a lot.) I have to admit I have a disability, which is an admission of weakness that doesn't come easy for me. So that's the "humility" I must experience every day.

Here's the beauty of how God works, though: I've found that when I admit I am weak, others jump in and complement my weakness with their strength. And that act of love touches me most when someone "strong" shows GENUINE HUMILITY.

One time during our travels, we disembarked our boat to walk into a remote New Guinea village that was ready to bedazzle us with their ornate costumes and body paint. A photographer's paradise! I know how much Thom loves to capture photographs, so I didn't mind slowly bringing up the rear. As I hobbled along, one of the ship's photographers kindly loaned her arm to help me. Her name was Sue Flood. Because I knew this was a once-in-lifetime visit to this location and she'd never been before, I told her to go on ahead. "No, that's okay. I can help you." How sweet! It wasn't until later that I learned she was a famous Australian photographer honored by the Queen of England for her extraordinary

work on BBC's *Planet Earth* video series. When someone you consider a "big shot" reaches out, it's jolting. Not unlike Jesus, God's Son, who humbled himself, joining us on this earthly journey.

Another example came from a woman on the other end of the spectrum. On the Pacific island country of Vanuatu we stayed in a primitive bamboo hut, eating meals in our host's small, darkened hut. Each day Abraham's wife slaved away to cook for us. Over mealtime conversations we learned our hosts were Christian. They invited us to church on Sunday. The dilemma for me? We had to hike quite a distance through the jungle, past the grassy airstrip, back into the jungle. But I was up for it. I'll never forget the kind, humble native woman who clutched my arm tightly as we walked along the way. "I'm sorry I'm slowing you down," I apologized. She leaned in and grabbed my arm tighter.

"It is my blessing," she said.

Wow! She viewed her act of serving as a blessing. Ever since, I've remembered her lesson to me. It *is* a blessing to be there for each other to offer love through GENUINE HUMILITY.

How to **PRACTICE LOVE WITH** Genuine **HUMILITY**

The following few pages list a variety of tips and principles that will help you love others through GENUINE HUMILITY. Like RADICAL HOSPITALITY and FEARLESS CONVERSATION, it takes practice. But every improvement you make in your attitude of GENUINE HUMILITY makes your personal Jesus-magnet stronger and stronger.

Be intentional about relationships.

To be genuinely humble, we must be like Jesus. We embody what God wants the world to see—Christians who care first and foremost about relationships. We need to be known as those who reach out to others as Jesus did. Sadly, instead of loving others, a great many Christians spend more of their time competing, complaining, campaigning, fighting, hiding, avoiding, bullying, shouting, protesting, and worse.

If there's anything you should be doing to strengthen your faith, it's making relationships a priority in your spiritual life. Be friends with the people God's leading you toward—your own family, co-workers, and neighbors. Communicate with them. Take time to be with them and listen to them, being fully present in their presence.

This is something that's greatly needed in our society, and Christians can be the ones to fill that need. Sociologists are shocked at what's been happening in our culture in recent years. Researchers found "the number of people saying there is no one with whom they discussed important matters nearly tripled" in 20 years. And "almost half of the population (43.6 percent) now [report] that they discuss important matters with either no one or with only one other person."[1] What a remarkable opportunity we have before us—to be there for all the people around us who need to talk about the big things in their lives.

Be intentionally with others.

In their book *Click*, authors Ori and Rom Brafman talk about three key components of being present. They tell a story about what one doctor learned about the first component, *intentionality:* "She needed to become present so that the patient felt seen and understood…[Intentionality] means entering an interaction with a sense of purpose and conscious awareness. Intentionality means giving the interaction our undivided attention, instead of going through the motions of being preoccupied with other things."[2]

128

The next component of presence is *mutuality:* being open and available to meet the other person where they are. Mutuality means focusing on the shared aspects of trust and honesty involved in a relationship, rather than giving advice or trying to solve a problem.

The third is what the Brafman brothers call *resonance:* "Resonance doesn't just make us feel more connected to our surroundings; research shows that at its core, resonance is contagious. We tend to match the emotions of those around us."[3]

Put simply, your loving presence with one another can be contagious. Remember, you're modeling Jesus to people. Jesus' love is contagious and others can experience it through you.

Model vulnerability.

We've found that when Christians share a slice of their own life, people are touched by that. One of our friends in children's ministry told us about a teacher who told the kids in her Sunday school class, "This morning I had a fight with my husband." The kids all gasped. The leader was being vulnerable. She said, "I didn't like that I was impatient. That's where I needed God to help me." In her vulnerability, the children realized it's possible for a real person to allow a real relationship with God to make a real difference in her life.

It's all about living in the truth. For so long we put on the appearance that we've got it all together. We all know no one has it all together this side of heaven.

We can't expect others to emotionally go places we ourselves aren't willing to go.

Are you willing to let down your defenses and expose your struggles and unanswered questions to those you're befriending? People will reciprocate your honesty and vulnerability over time. Honest, humble believers have the potential to make a profound impact on the relationships in their lives.

If you want others to open up and be vulnerable, set the example. If you want a friend to talk about how hard it's been to forgive someone in their life, you go first.

Ori and Rom Brafman also talk about the benefits of vulnerability in their book *Click*: "In terms of creating an instant connection, vulnerability and self-disclosure are, in fact, strengths…When we interact with people with whom we've formed an instant connection, we tend to give each other the benefit of the doubt. The trust that forms gives us permission to disagree, because we know that our counterpart will support us emotionally, even if we diverge in our opinions."[4]

Resolve conflict biblically.

It's inevitable that you will encounter conflict when trying to show love to others. It will put your GENUINE HUMILITY to the test. But those difficult moments may be your greatest opportunities to prove your love and let Jesus shine through you.

Our friend and co-worker Bob D'Ambrosio compiled this wonderful checklist of things you can do to work through conflicts and disagreements with others. You'll allow Scripture to work through your life and let your GENUINE HUMILITY do the heavy lifting.

1. Examine yourself. Before you get involved, take a close look at your heart, motives, and attitudes to make sure they're in tune with Scripture. (Matthew 7:1-5)

2. Try to settle matters immediately, but privately. Don't involve crowds of people who really don't need to be involved. (Matthew 5:23-24; 18:15-17)

3. Avoid needless conflict or arguments. Instead, encourage collaboration and cooperation, Jesus-style. (2 Timothy 2:23-26)

4. Think about the situation and the most appropriate response before you speak. A calm response often diffuses the situation, but a sarcastic or heated response just ratchets up the anger levels. (Proverbs 15:1-2, 23)

5. Speak the truth in love. When Jesus confronted someone, he didn't list the person's sins. He just had a FEARLESS CONVERSATION with that person, and by the end of their chat that person recognized their failings on their own. (Ephesians 4:14-16, 25-28; John 4:7-26)

6. Seek peace and grace. The ultimate goal of resolving disputes is to build each other up spiritually. We need to go beyond ending the harsh words and feelings and replace them with words that affirm each other. (Romans 14:19; Ephesians 4:29-32)

7. Leave the conflict in the past. Just as God blots out the record of our sins, we need to forgive. Love and forgiveness are inseparable throughout Scripture. (1 Corinthians 13:5; Job 14:16-17; Proverbs 17:9)

Let people know you're thinking of them.

Perhaps this may sound obvious, but when you send a kind card, email, or text, you're letting others know that you're not putting yourself first. You're telling others, "I've been spending some of my time thinking about you and caring about you."

Don't wait to send that note. When it pops into your head, take five minutes and let that person know they're in your thoughts and prayers. In our opinion, handwritten notes are the best surprise, but even a quick text can be all a person needs to get through a tough situation or bring a smile to their day.

Beware of using the bait and switch.

People not connected to God have a keen ability to detect this. Those who don't see value in Jesus or Christians are doubly suspicious of invitations or relationships that seem inauthentic.

When she was in college, our daughter-in-law was invited to coffee by a well-meaning campus minister. It didn't take long for her to realize he wasn't really interested in her as a person; he was trying to gain another notch in his spiritual belt. He spouted lots of Scripture and frowned at her lack of in-depth Bible knowledge. It left a sour taste in her mouth, even though she was already a believer. Needless to say, she didn't attend any more of that campus ministry's meetings. They simply weren't humbly interested in growing relationships.

People in authentic relationships are in them for the long haul. And they're in them for the right reasons. The campus minister didn't live up to the common expectation of what it means to meet a friend for coffee. When you want to build a relationship, do what a real friend would do.

Don't merely tolerate people.

Our local conversation café attracts a great assortment of interesting people. One of our favorites is Joe. He's a wild-haired, retired professor who actively contributes to our discussions. "I'm a raging liberal," he loves to say. One of our hot topics brought up the subject of tolerance. Joe raised his hand. "I don't want to be tolerated," he said. "Who wants to be 'tolerated'? I want to be accepted."

His comment struck deep. With all our culture's talk of tolerance, that's not really what people long for: We want to be welcomed and loved.

Give people *real* respect and *real* love. Joe was right—no one wants to be tolerated. Never once did Jesus command us to "tolerate one another as I have tolerated you."

When we say something offensive like "Love the sinner but hate the sin," (which we've been guilty of) we're implying that we're going to spend half our time hating something about that person and who they are. Christians have a reputation for being intolerant, and many Christians respond by saying, "Of course I'm intolerant! I'm intolerant of sin!" But there's nothing humble about that overcharged response. Nor does it help us maintain a mindset of love toward those we think we need to be so "tolerant" of.

Tom Nelson, author of *Work Matters*, puts it this way: "When we live a life of common grace, we are not soft on sin or apathetic toward wrongdoing, nor are we a doormat of passivity for people to walk over, but we find contentment in our hearts that God is in charge, and he is the one who will settle any scores that need to be settled."[5]

Let go of your right to be right.

This seems to be the most difficult touchpoint for a lot of Christians. You see this every day in online social networks. Bible-quoting Christians hammer their convictions again and again into conversations on Facebook and Twitter about any number of issues. It's sad and frustrating and serves only to fuel the reputation Christians have for being judgmental, uncaring, and hypocritical.

We're intrigued by what Pope Francis said about the church's unhealthy obsession with focusing on rules rather than people. "We have to find a new balance; otherwise even the moral edifice of the church is likely to fall like a house of cards, losing the freshness and fragrance of the Gospel," Francis said.

Even when it comes to big issues like homosexuality and abortion, the pope discourages the upholding of doctrine as the church's priority: "The teaching of the church...is clear...but it is not necessary to talk about these issues all the time."[6]

What do we really care about? Defending our beliefs? Defending God? Defending our political and religious rights? Defending our judgmental behavior? So much defense is, frankly, offensive.

We can do better. GENUINE HUMILITY says, "I don't have to be right. Sure, I have my beliefs, and I'm happy to talk about them. But I'll still love you and treat you with respect no matter how much we disagree. And I won't belittle or condemn you for your beliefs."

Share your questions.

When I (Joani) was talking with Chris (who, as a 9-year-old, never went back to church because he asked too many questions), he practically leapt from his chair when I said I have questions too.

"Say that! If Christians would say they have questions too, I'd have so much more respect for them," Chris told me.

We do indeed have questions and doubts. We're not sure we'd believe you if you said you didn't.

People are abandoning the church because Christians won't allow honest dialogue and questions. God does not fear questions. God can handle them. One time our friend and co-worker Tamara came to us, saddened.

132

She had just interviewed a bright couple who, just years before, had been devout believers. They were active members of a robust, faith-based campus organization. But eventually their relentless Bible memorization and witnessing turned sour because no one in the organization would let them ask questions. Honest, hard, grappling questions about the Bible, gnarly issues about sexuality, mysterious questions about the supernatural world, science, and religion. We must allow people, within the context of faith relationships, to wrestle with even the most difficult of questions. Even the ones without great answers.

Let your actions speak for you.

An amazing thing is happening in our world right now as people watch Pope Francis. They're watching the pope even more than listening to him. His actions of GENUINE HUMILITY magnetize the world to him. He lives in a humble abode, he stands up for his predecessor, he visits prisons and washes prisoners' feet, and he even gets miffed that the media boasts about his humility. He doesn't want a fanfare; he simply wants to serve, live, and love like Jesus. It's so, so refreshing.

GENUINE HUMILITY is a rare commodity in our world—especially, it seems, among Christians.

People are watching us. All the time. It can be intimidating and scary to know our lives speak louder than our words. Yet this may be the biggest opportunity of all that God has placed before us. As a Jesus-follower, we can live a life (with God's help) that glows love. Shoveling someone's driveway, volunteering to take a neighbor's kids to school, helping instead of complaining about the school system, speaking kindly of others instead of gossiping.

Let's let the fruit of the Spirit—love, joy, peace, patience, kindness, goodness, self-control—speak for us.

133

It can be helpful to understand what the fruit of the Spirit looks and sounds like in our lives when we identify their opposites:

Living the Love of God	Living the Opposite
Love	Hate
Joy	Frowning cynicism
Peace	Feeling unsettled or agitated
Patience	Impatience
Kindness	Being mean-spirited or a bully
Goodness	Thinking only of ourselves
Self-control	Out of control

> "But the Holy Spirit produces this kind of fruit in our lives: **LOVE, JOY, PEACE, PATIENCE, KINDNESS, GOODNESS, FAITHFULNESS, GENTLENESS, AND SELF-CONTROL.** There is no law against these things."
>
> —Galatians 5:22-23

Seek to understand.

Catch yourself and use your "Arrogance Alert" when you feel yourself beginning to think, "This other person is an idiot. If only they knew what I know...." Today when others say Christians are hypocrites, it's not so much that their actions or words don't match. Here's what they're really saying: "You're so arrogant. And I know you don't know everything."

We must drop our "holier than thou" or "smarter than thou" attitudes and admit we really don't know everything. Belief isn't the same as omnipotence. That's why we need faith.

Share the unlimited grace God has given you.

Sometime we greatly underestimate the damage our lack of GENUINE HUMILITY can cause. Our friend Deb shared this with us:

"One of the toughest times in my life was when the pastor of my church exposed himself as the most hypocritical of all the Christians I knew. I was a full-time volunteer on his staff and saw and heard many things I wish I hadn't. But the thing that changed everything for me was when he fired our youth pastor for a past sin committed many years before, when he was just 21. This youth leader was humble and had admitted his mistake to his youth group. He had brought almost 300 young people to Christ through his ministry.

"When our youth pastor was let go, almost all the kids lost their respect for the church and stopped going. My kids included. I was heartbroken but didn't blame them. Where was the grace our pastor had preached about from the stage each Sunday? The church split after that and more than half left, disillusioned and questioning their faith instead of the man who was our leader. Thank God that youth leader continued to mentor many of those kids, and many went back to church before they left for college."

Dim the Christian "stars."

Perhaps it can't be helped that some Christians become famous. Authors, singers, megachurch pastors, speakers, bloggers, and others have become celebrities for Christians. We've had our fair share of interaction with many of them over the years. Some of them are authentically lovely people. For many, fame has eaten away at their GENUINE HUMILITY.

We won't belabor this point, but we strongly encourage people not to drool over Christian celebrities. It's unhealthy. It doesn't grow your faith. It doesn't bring you closer to God. Shine your spotlight on Jesus.

Celebrities fail. Jesus never fails.

135

Pray for your enemies.

This is a tough one. We've had our share of adversaries and antagonists. During our 40 years in the business world, there have been times when we've had to let staff go, and it happens for a variety of reasons. Some people get angry. Some of them have come to hate us. They've threatened us. Called us names. But Jesus-style love calls us to pray for them. It's never easy. But it works. They don't know we're praying for them, but it softens our hearts so we can leave the rest up to God.

Shattering the Obstacles

GENUINE HUMILITY is utterly powerful because it puts everything in God's control. When we're able to admit that we don't have all the answers, that our lives are not perfect, and that we still have so much to learn, then we're finally ready to love through GENUINE HUMILITY. It's an irresistible act of love because it's so authentic. It makes Jesus' love infinitely magnetic because it drops virtually all the barriers that Christians have put up between themselves and nonbelievers.

We have one more act of love to cover: DIVINE ANTICIPATION. Are you ready for what God has in store?

Endnotes

1. Miller McPherson, Lynn Smith-Lovin, and Matthew E. Brashears, "Social Isolation in America: Changes in Core Discussion Networks over Two Decades," *American Sociological Review,* Vol. 71 (2006), 353.

2. Ori Brafman and Rom Brafman, *Click* (New York, NY: Broadway Books, 2010), 88.

3. Ibid., 90.

4. Ibid., 32, 178-179.

5. Tom Nelson, *Work Matters: Connecting Sunday Worship to Monday Work* (Wheaton, IL: Crossway, 2011), 135.

6. Pope Francis, quoted in Nicole Winfield and Rachel Zoll, "Pope: Church will fail if mired in rules for gays, abortion," MSN News, September 19, 2013, http://news.msn.com/world/pope-church-will-fail-if-mired-in-rules-for-gays-abortion.

7 DIVINE ANTICIPATION

Sometimes when you **EXPECT GOD TO DO HIS WORK,** your very life may be on the line.

Our friend Nathan knows that firsthand. He's a cop.

He's seen things on the job that would make you cringe. He's found himself in the line of gunfire. He recently lost a fellow officer—a dear friend—who killed himself. That was the sixth suicide in the police force in recent years. The nightmares in Nathan's life are real.

You'd like Nathan instantly if you met him. He loves God with all his heart. And he loves his fellow officers with all his heart. His humility is genuine, and his hunger to introduce people to Jesus is as real as it gets. He's the kind of Christian who'd rather spend his time actively showing love to people who need it than sitting in a pew while they struggle.

It's hard to believe such a good guy like Nathan is someone who faces human horrors on a regular basis. But when he practices love through DIVINE ANTICIPATION, truly amazing things have happened.

One day while on duty, Nathan and another officer (also a Christian) received a call about a domestic dispute between a husband, his wife, and their 20-year-old daughter. The father was drunk, as he was virtually every day, and his rage had turned violent.

When they arrived on the scene, Nathan confronted the man about what had happened. The man's anger intensified, and he threatened to kill the officers. Nathan tried to de-escalate the situation, but the man lunged to the kitchen to grab a 12-inch knife.

Nathan had his gun ready.

But the man paused. "I want to kill myself," he said.

Nathan also paused. He could sense a deep well of hurt inside the man. His DIVINE ANTICIPATION kicked into action. "I prayed for Kingdom eyes because my flesh wanted to punch him in the face for punching his daughter in the face," he admitted. The Holy Spirit answered his prayer.

"I asked a wondering question about how he felt inside about the situation," Nathan said. "He broke. He started weeping and sat down on the floor."

They took the man to the hospital for a psychological evaluation. Nathan and his partner took turns praying and ministering to him—the man who had threatened to kill them. The man talked about his disbelief and anger with God. Again, Nathan felt led to ask him more wondering questions. Nathan wondered if he really didn't believe in God…or if he was running from the reality of God and his love. Again, the man broke into tears.

Nathan told us he wasn't sure if he should share his faith in Jesus with the man. But when they stepped out of the hospital room for a few minutes to pray, his partner said he could tell God's Spirit wanted Nathan to tell his story. Nathan still had his share of doubts, but he could sense the Holy Spirit working.

"Tag, your turn," his partner said.

His DIVINE ANTICIPATION had brought them this far, and Nathan knew he should keep depending on God to act. He knew he needed to keep loving the man who had threatened to end his life only hours earlier.

With the doctors and nurses out of the room, Nathan sat down with the man. Several more wondering questions later, Nathan was vulnerable and told him about his own personal relationship with God—how he, too, had struggled with suicidal thoughts and how God had met him at his lowest point in life. Amazingly, the broken man asked God to come into his life and take control.

"His prayer was so raw and beautiful," Nathan told us.

They all hugged and called each other "brother."

(For more of Nathan's compelling story, watch our documentary, *When God Left the Building*. Find information at WhenGodLeftTheBuilding.com.)

LOOKING for GOD

Nathan will be the first to tell you that he had his share of doubts throughout that situation (and many others). He would be the last person on earth to call himself any kind of a spiritual hero. But he would say that acting in love—through DIVINE ANTICIPATION—is something God does through him and his life as a police officer. He expects God to show up, and God does.

It's astonishing to us how many Christians don't seem to anticipate that God will be obviously active in their daily lives. We've found that many people of faith have a difficult time seeing what God is really doing among them—his church. Thankfully, sometimes we get to watch as the light—or, more accurately, the Light—turns on for people who finally understand how real God is. We call that DIVINE ANTICIPATION.

We met Giovy a couple of years ago when she attended one of our ministry training events. We were surprised she was there, as she was one of the most skeptical people we'd ever met. She sat in the back of the room, arms crossed, and challenged the premise of what we were teaching.

But what happened next changed her life. During an experience we called "Is God Real?" we gave instructions for everyone to find a partner— someone they didn't know very well—and then each person would close their eyes for a full minute and listen to God to see if he had a message for their partner. The message may come in the form of a mental picture...a phrase...a Scripture reference...anything.

Giovy paired up with someone she didn't know (who happened to be a pastor's wife), and she thought, "Okay, God, give me *something* good because here's this pastor's wife and she's a spiritual person.'" The only thing that came to mind was an image of bamboo. And she thought, "Come on God; give me something." But the idea in her mind didn't change; it was still bamboo. She thought, "This is the weirdest thing."

When the minute was over, she got back with her partner who shared what God had showed her for Giovy. It was a beautiful spiritual thing. Then the pastor's wife asked, "What did God show you for me?" Giovy replied, "I don't even want to say. I'm really embarrassed. All I saw was... bamboo." The pastor's wife sat back in her chair, the color draining from her face, eyes tearing up. Giovy thought, "What did I say?" The woman then said, "Two weeks ago I was reading a devotional about the bamboo tree and how it's a very strong tree, but it's also very flexible. I feel that I need to be more flexible, and that devotion pointed out the thing that I need to work on. I'm working on it; God is working on me. That devotional has been in my head for the last two weeks. And now you say the word *bamboo.*" They were both thinking, "Wow! This is incredible! Only God can do this!"

A few weeks later back at home, Giovy received a package from the pastor's wife. She opened the box that had "live" written on it. Inside was a bamboo shoot. (It's now over two feet tall!)

Giovy told us, "I have grown more in the last two years…than in 43 years of my Christian walk. I realized I was pushing people away. I realized that faith is a process. I am a changed person."

She truly is a different person than she was two years ago, and now she is able to see for herself how active God is in her life and the lives of the people around her. Her faith has become a relationship.

WHAT'S So Compelling About DIVINE ANTICIPATION?

Perhaps the most powerful and mysterious act of love is DIVINE ANTICIPATION. We can't fully understand or explain in human terms what happens when it happens. But it does.

DIVINE ANTICIPATION isn't a freaky, weird way to live. It's actually quite natural for us to tune into the supernatural. It's living in the mystery and wonder of God.

More than ever, our culture has squeezed our understanding of life into measurable facts, figures, analysis, scientific tidbits, technology, and cold, hard proof. Yet God still manages to overtake us. We can't make the sun shine or the rain fall. We can't bring a body to life, and we can't explain how the world came to be and how it keeps spinning. From the incomprehensible, overwhelming nature of the universe to the tiniest forms of life, our world still holds mystery. And the mystery is most profound when it's played out in every stage of our lives—birth, death, relationships, achievement, loss, joy, sorrow, questions, and answers.

That said, DIVINE ANTICIPATION means we emphasize God's reality, presence, and action in our lives today. He is amazing, incredible, and wonderful *now*. Christians have done a great job of emphasizing God's might throughout history; all those Sunday school classes and Bible studies point us to the God of history in Bible times. We need to remember every day, every hour that God is as awesome today as ever.

140

We're calling for a movement that not only celebrates the acts of God recorded in the Bible but equally emphasizes what God is doing today. DIVINE ANTICIPATION invites and trains people to watch for God in action today. To live with the understanding that "God is here, ready to connect with you in a fresh way" is utterly transformative.

> "So the Word became human and made his home among us. He was full of unfailing love and faithfulness. **AND WE HAVE SEEN HIS GLORY, THE GLORY OF THE FATHER'S ONE AND ONLY SON.**"
>
> —John 1:14

JESUS-STYLE Divine Anticipation

Jesus lived a life of DIVINE ANTICIPATION. His whole purpose fulfilled God's will, and he fully expected God with his every breath.

God's Son also gave us clues for how to live in DIVINE ANTICIPATION. Perhaps the time in Jesus' life when he may have been most anticipatory was just before his crucifixion. What did it mean for him to live totally connected to God the Father?

Put yourself in this scene. You've just experienced a foot washing and a meal of bread and wine. Jesus gave new meaning to the food and drink. Then Jesus said something about someone betraying him. Craziness. Everything is madly swirling around in your head and heart. What's going on? Nothing makes sense. What's happening? Then...

"As soon as Judas left the room, Jesus said, 'The time has come for the Son of Man to enter into his glory, and God will be glorified because of him. And since God receives glory because of the Son, he will soon give glory to the Son...So now I am giving you a new commandment: Love each other. Just as I have loved you, you should love each other. Your love for one another will prove to the world that you are my disciples'" (John 13:31-35).

141

In this unsettling time, Jesus points to love. An act of God's ultimate love about to unfold with arms outstretched upon a cross.

Jesus paved the way for us. And now we can bring God's glory in human form through love. What a brilliant plan! Instead of hardened, unmovable stone temples, he designed people—*us*—to be his living temples pointing others to God by loving them.

The rest is history. His story plus our story. A love story.

As we, the church, strive to live our calling, maybe, just maybe, we can love more deeply.

Because of Jesus.

> And this is the secret: **CHRIST LIVES IN YOU.**
>
> —Colossians 1:27

How to Recognize **DIVINE ANTICIPATION**

Perhaps it goes without saying, but we'll say it anyway. The first step toward understanding and seeing DIVINE ANTICIPATION in action is to trust the Holy Spirit. If we're open to fresh ways of encountering God, we know that the Spirit will work through us and show us God's hand in virtually every aspect of our lives. Trusting the Holy Spirit means truly letting go of our own agendas and allowing God to do his work. That's really what DIVINE ANTICIPATION is all about.

When we talk about DIVINE ANTICIPATION, here's what we mean:

Realizing God is actively involved all the time.

Like radio waves, we just need to tune in. We expectantly trust, believe, hope, and know God is at work. Perhaps the greatest flaw is creating a sacred/secular divide.

God is alive today. We see him in our daily decisions, in nature, a new baby, or an act of kindness. God is all around us. God is alive and real. He is active. Here. Now. But most people don't know for sure that he's really there. Not that they don't know about Jesus. They just think he's dead.

Eugene Peterson expressed it beautifully in *Eat This Book*: "[God] is present, often unnoticed, frequently anonymous, among actual men and women located in time and place, in the context of their ancestors and in the towns and valleys and mountains in which they had all grown up. And there's a lot more stories of the same sort. These are the stories that formed Israel's imagination—quiet, everyday, the supernatural camouflaged in the natural, the presence of God revealed in the places and among the people involved in our day to day living."[1]

God *is* real. It's just that people have forgotten to notice.

Grasping God's power.

We need to fully understand that the power that brought Jesus back from the dead is the same power working in and through us. That's supernatural power! Like Paul, this is our prayer: "I [we] also pray that you will understand the incredible greatness of God's power for us who believe him. This is the same mighty power that raised Christ from the dead and seated him in the place of honor at God's right hand in the heavenly realms" (Ephesians 1:19-20).

Putting the 4 ACTS OF LOVE into practice is possible when we trust God is working through us every day, just as he promised.

Dive into those words! What incredible God-adventure awaits you? Do we believe this enough to take the plunge?

> "I tell you the truth, anyone who believes in me will do the same works I have done, and even greater works, because I am going to be with the Father. **YOU CAN ASK FOR ANYTHING IN MY NAME, AND I WILL DO IT, SO THAT THE SON CAN BRING GLORY TO THE FATHER.** Yes, ask me for anything in my name, and I will do it!"
> —John 14:12-14

143

Accepting there are things we just can't explain.

That's what faith is all about. It doesn't mean you check your brains at the door or don't enjoy the world's ever-growing bank of discoveries. It means coming to grips with our human nature, which isn't divine. We are not God.

That's why we trust the Holy Spirit.

It's dangerous and scary, and it goes against everything our culture teaches. But to trust the Holy Spirit means that we can't cling so tightly to our plans.

> The inspiration arrives in a rough, bumpy, and earthy language that reveals God's presence and action where we least expect it, catching us when we are up to our elbows in the soiled ordinariness of our culture and when spiritual thoughts are the furthest thing from our minds.[2]
> —Eugene Peterson, *Eat This Book*

Being relevant—and realizing that God is relevant to everyone.

A lot of Christians confuse being relevant with being hip or cool or contemporary. It's not. Tamie Harkins, former chaplain for Canterbury Fellowship at Northern Arizona University describes it this way (she's talking about the church; translated, us):

"A few words on relevancy: making your church hip and trendy (coffee bar; free wireless; pastor with tattoos and ripped jeans) will probably draw in the young people. If your only goal is getting young people in the door, these things will work. Free alcohol will work even better (I guess you could advertise the Eucharist that way...). I don't have a problem with coffee, wireless, tattoos or ripped jeans, or thimble-size sips of alcohol. It's just that, what do these things have to do with being relevant? Relevancy is about practices and conversations that address people's pressing and real concerns. Relevancy is about offering practices that help people come to peace with the death of someone they love. Relevancy is conversation about global warming and extreme poverty...Relevancy also means looking around the community and the world, noticing who's marginalized and oppressed—because that's where Jesus put his attention—and finding ways to stand with and for those people. This 'finding ways' is where the sole meets the trail, and that's where we've got to think creatively together."[3]

144

Expecting God to show up.

Our friend Nathan had no idea what would happen when he confronted the man holding a knife in the kitchen. His hand may have been on the tip of his gun handle, but his heart was waiting on God. As afraid as he was, Nathan expected God to show up.

If we adopt DIVINE ANTICIPATION as one of our key strategies for loving others, then we absolutely must expect God to show up, even if—or, especially when—everything seems to be on the line.

Now, expecting God to show up doesn't necessarily mean that God will do what we expect him to. More often than not, God has much better things in mind.

On a recent trip to Thailand, we met a boy named Peng. We were there to film his story for a children's ministry project. Before the sun rose, our film crew captured 11-year-old Peng groggily crawl out of his wooden plank bunk bed. He lived among 40 other orphans whose parents chose to leave them in someone else's care. For whatever reasons, these parents could not bear the burden of raising a child.

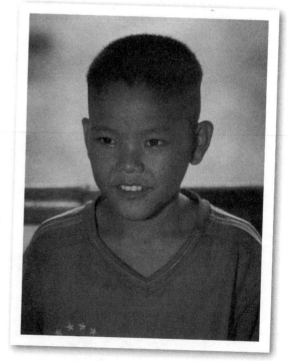

We realized quickly that Peng was a stoic kid, not the perky, happy-go-lucky boy we had hoped to record. In fact, his serious expression made us think we'd made a big mistake. He was a reluctant subject to say the

145

least. He barely looked up as he robotically slurped up his noodle breakfast on his tin plate. He quietly allowed—more like tolerated—our cameras to follow him. Yet even as we climbed with him aboard the makeshift school bus, he looked straight ahead, strong but joyless.

Our plan had been to capture a day in Peng's life at school. While the other girls and boys squirmed and giggled, he remained somber. He seemed embarrassed that our film crew was focused on him. Again, we wondered if we were making a mistake. But we couldn't escape the feeling that God had something special planned. We'd seen God show up before on countless occasions; surely we could expect God to show up again.

After filming his 5th-grade English class, we left the school for a break. Unbeknownst to us, this day was the big "Sports Day" at the nearby high school. We were instantly enraptured by the event—costumes, marching bands, cheerleaders, athletes and teams in colors galore—a mini Olympic-like extravaganza. It was the kind of stuff film crews live for. This, we were certain, was our God-sent surprise for the day. Perhaps this was that special something God had orchestrated for our day—not the cheerless boy named Peng.

We went back to Peng's school at lunchtime to find the typical carefree nature of an elementary school campus. We filmed so many happy children that afternoon, trying to make the most of our day we thought had been all but a loss. Peng was nowhere in sight. We joked that he was probably hiding somewhere to avoid our cameras. Little did we know that Peng's story would end up being the one thing that took our breath away.

Thankfully, God was in control, not us.

WHY NOBODY WANTS TO BE AROUND CHRISTIANS ANYMORE

We met up with Peng after school at the orphanage. We were determined to get him to open up to us at least a little, perhaps get him to show us what made him happy, if anything. We had been warned not to bring up his parents. The director told us the weight of abandonment was too much for his innocent young heart.

We followed Peng to his locker, a small closet containing his clothes and a few little treasures.

"Show us what you have in your locker," we asked as cheerfully as we could through the interpreter.

Peng's expression didn't change. "I have nothing," he said. But then… he cracked a smile as he unzipped a DVD pouch containing a few movies of his favorite Chinese fighter show. Then he put on a red soccer T-shirt. "Someday he wants to be a football star," the translator said. Peng proceeded to show us his few other possessions—erasers, plastic trucks, and a few action figures. At last we saw a glimpse of the little boy hidden behind the grim face. He then pulled out his pocket-size Thai Bible and read us a passage about Jesus feeding many people. Then he solemnly tucked everything back in his pouch and zipped it shut.

We set up outside for Peng's final interview around a bamboo table and bench. I (Joani) thought I'd start with an "easy" question: "Tell us what are your favorite things?" I asked with the brightest smile I could muster. I was determined to cheer him up somehow.

"My mother and father," he said.

We were stunned and didn't know what to say. He brought up the one topic we weren't supposed to talk about.

"I don't know them," Peng continued. "But their memory is in my heart."

The interpreter and I tried hard to hold back our tears. We now understood Peng's expression of stone. Here was a young boy who was haunted by parents he never knew. He loves them, but they didn't love him back.

My judgmental attitude about this somber child changed in an instant. It was a challenge to compose ourselves and continue the interview. Even the interpreter later admitted that his words were too touching and difficult for her to translate.

We tried to veer back into cheerful territory. More questions about his favorite animals, his best friend, soccer—all the things that brought him happiness. But eventually I hit another question on my list: "What makes you sad?"

"Today is my mother's birthday," Peng said, his expression as stoic as ever. "I wish I could sing her a song."

That day, of all days, was the hardest day in Peng's life. We had crossed paths with him at a time when he was feeling the deepest sorrow in his heart.

We had focused on the all-too-serious side of this kind, hard-working, responsible boy. He did his daily chores, scrubbing the latrine and washing clothes, with barely a sigh. He shared his snacks, never looking selfish for even a moment. Despite his dark history, he was making peace by appreciating the orphanage and giving back in whatever way he could. And he told us that he knows Jesus is always with him.

He most certainly is.

Once we know someone's story, it's practically impossible to judge them and even harder to withhold love from them.

And when you fully expect God to show up, he will.

Trusting that God will do what only God can do.

We are in a miraculous partnership with God who allows us to plant, water, and cultivate "seeds." But God is the one who makes things grow. I (Joani) grew up on a farm and know the difference between the farmer's job and God's job. As much as humans work at planting and harvesting crops, farmers cannot make a plant grow. It's a miracle. Christians often try so hard to make things happen the way we feel is best. But, instead, we need to step back more often and watch God make our efforts grow.

"After all, who is Apollos? Who is Paul? We are only God's servants through whom you believed the Good News. Each of us did the work the Lord gave us. I planted the seed in your hearts, and Apollos watered it, but it was God who made it grow. It's not important who does the planting, or who does the watering. **WHAT'S IMPORTANT IS THAT GOD MAKES THE SEED GROW.**" —1 Corinthians 3:5-7

We marvel at our friend Candace's love toward one couple and her trust in God, knowing that he works everything out in his timing. Candace's love is the love of DIVINE ANTICIPATION. Her attitude and actions put into practice how the Holy Spirit works. Galatians 5:22-23 says it like this: "The Holy Spirit produces this kind of fruit in our lives: love, joy, peace, patience, kindness, goodness, faithfulness, gentleness, and self-control."

See what we mean. In Candace's own words...

Our friendship has endured for nearly three decades. Joseph and Bella have shared my sorrow at the deaths of my stepdad and grandmother, and I've shared theirs when Joseph's parents died. A few years after we met, they moved across the country, but we've always remained in touch.

Joseph is Jewish and was raised in an orthodox home, but he holds to his Judaism loosely. Bella was raised in a nominally Christian home, but over years of searching for spiritual truth, she has come to embrace Hinduism.

Five years ago, after accepting a powerful position and moving to a new city, Joseph was diagnosed with a rare, usually fatal disease. In the last five years, he and Bella have suffered indignities and pain I can only imagine. Because this happened shortly after they'd moved, they've had no close friends nearby, so they've largely been alone.

Feeling powerless to help in any meaningful way, I decided to at least call Bella once a week, just to check in, listen to the cries of her heart, and remind her that I love her. Several months ago, during a long conversation in which I felt overwhelmed by the crushing weight of all they're facing, I asked if she minded if I prayed with her—something I'd never done before. She gladly and readily agreed and, afterward, cried as she thanked me.

The next day, I received this email from her:

I want to take a few minutes to share with you what happened after we hung up yesterday. I was once again very moved by your prayer and carried it with me around the house as I began to get busy. After a few minutes, I stopped in my tracks as a tingling had started in my heels. As I stood there, it turned to goose bumps and some shivering and started traveling up my legs, then my back, then into the back of my head, then out the top of my head. I started to panic, but then I thought to ask, "Is this you, God? Letting me know you are real and that Candace's pray has power?" And he said, "Yes, I just wanted you to be sure to feel my presence." Then today as I meditated, I had a sense that things with us had shifted for the better. Hope this lifts your day, sweet friend, as it lifted mine.

Here's my response:

Oh, Bella, this gives me goose bumps! I am thrilled and awed by God's loving intervention into your heart, mind, and even body yesterday. I can't thank you adequately for sharing this with me. I believe with all my heart that God is drawing you and Joseph closer to him with each passing day, that he longs for you to know him for who he truly is, to experience his love and his peace, which truly does surpass all understanding. Don't ever hesitate to call me. It doesn't matter whether I'm at home, at work, or somewhere in between. If I'm in a meeting and can't answer, just leave a message. I always, always, always love to hear your voice.

A few days later, I felt moved to send her this, as it spoke so perfectly of her situation:

" 'To whom will you compare me? Or who is my equal?' says the Holy One. Lift up your eyes and look to the heavens: Who created all these? He who brings out the starry host one by one and calls forth each of them by name. Because of his great power and mighty strength, not one of them is missing. Why do you complain, Jacob? Why do you say, Israel, 'My way is hidden from the Lord; my cause is disregarded by my God'? Do you not know? Have you not heard? The Lord is the everlasting God, the Creator of the ends of the earth. He will not grow tired or weary, and his understanding no one can fathom. He gives strength to the weary and increases the power of the weak. Even youths grow tired and weary, and young men stumble and fall; but those who hope in the Lord will renew their strength. They will soar on wings like eagles; they will run and not grow weary, they will walk and not be faint" (Isaiah 40:25-31, NIV).

The following week, during our weekly call, Bella asked me to pray again. And the following day, I received this email from her:

After you prayed for us on Monday, I had another experience that I thought you would appreciate. I had planned on getting up and getting busy as soon as we finished our phone call but decided to sit for a few more moments to savor your prayer. As I shut my eyes to linger there, I felt myself being lifted up. I looked down to see that I was leaving a morass of dark yuckiness (if there is such a word). I remembered Joseph all of a sudden and went to him quite worried. But he was also being lifted over darkness. And the sense has remained all week. And we really need this! Thanks for your miraculous prayers and God's infinite grace.

And here's my response:

Darling Bella, your words fill me with joy. God is at work in you and through you. There's a much bigger story being written here. I'm sure of it. I'm praying for you and Joseph at every opportunity. I love you so!

Since then, we've had more conversations about the nature of God, the existence of Satan and evil, the purpose of suffering. And these have been genuine, give-and-take conversations—with both of us asking questions like "What do you think?" "How did you come to that conclusion?" and "How has that changed your ability to cope?" and really listening to each other's responses.

Bella and Joseph's story is still being written. I don't know when or how their lives on this earth will come to an end. But I do know this: Our lives intersected for a reason. Our love for one another has endured over time and distance. It has deepened through hardship and suffering. God is at work, drawing these marvelous, generous, brilliant, loving souls near to him. And, after 28 years of friendship, it has been a privilege to speak of my faith to them—when asked and with respect for their beliefs.

That's DIVINE ANTICIPATION.

Telling others—in an authentic, natural way—what God is doing in our own lives and the lives of others.

When we as Christians start sharing what God is doing every day in our lives, we invite others to participate in our DIVINE ANTICIPATION. Not in a preachy sort of way, but in a natural, "oh, by-the-way" sort of way.

But Christians have turned evangelism into a scary prospect—it's become a sales pitch, or a dire warning, or an invitation to a secret club. We hold courses and sermons on what to say and how to do it. Regular people are afraid they'll say the wrong thing. After all, they're not the ministry "professionals."

There's a much better way. God has equipped us with his Holy Spirit simply to tell our own story—the good, the bad, and the real. The best part is no one can argue with us. It's our story. And when others realize you don't need a degree in evangelism, they become empowered to tell their own God-story. It's not that complicated. Maybe the early church thrived because they didn't pay people to be the professional "church people"—they all were "it."

Allowing people to express their faith in their own way.

How often do we interpret someone's inner thoughts from their outer expression? Every one of us has a singularly unique set of experiences. We each have an individual relationship with God that's truly distinct from every other Christian's. There's no one right way to express our faith, and we need—we must—allow for there to be differences in how the Holy Spirit shows up in our lives.

> "I want them to be encouraged and knit together by strong ties of love. **I WANT THEM TO HAVE COMPLETE CONFIDENCE THAT THEY UNDERSTAND GOD'S MYSTERIOUS PLAN, WHICH IS CHRIST HIMSELF.**"
>
> —Colossians 2:2

HOW TO PRACTICE LOVE Through Divine Anticipation

So what exactly can we say and do when it comes to DIVINE ANTICIPATION? Sure, hospitality and conversations seem so doable and practical, but how do we train ourselves to see the spiritual in our everyday lives as Christians?

Loving others through DIVINE ANTICIPATION isn't mysterious. It's something we can all do all the time with anyone.

The next few pages offer some hands-on things you can do to make DIVINE ANTICIPATION work in your daily Christian life. These are actions that we've witnessed again and again, and we can tell you they really, truly work. We've even provided real-life stories for each of them so you can see how they really make a difference in people's lives.

Expecting God and allowing him to reach and speak into your unique circle of relationships with others is a remarkable, amazing, unforgettable act of love.

Look for God Sightings.

One of the most fulfilling skills you can hone as a Christian is watching for and sharing what God is doing in your life and in the lives of those around you. Sharing our stories with each other is a way to experience faith as a living, breathing relationship.

We can't have a relationship with an expired historical figure. We *can* have a relationship with the living God who shows up through people and the events in their lives. God Sightings are a way for us to see God in action all around us. Anyone, from preschoolers to grandparents, can share God Sightings.

The problem is that it's so easy for us to miss the obvious.

Even the experts can miss things in plain sight, as demonstrated in a recent study conducted by Trafton Drew, a researcher at Harvard Medical School. Drew was familiar with the "Invisible Gorilla" study, in which people are shown a video of a group of kids passing a ball back and forth. The research subjects are asked to focus on counting the number of times the ball is passed, but about half of them don't see a man in a gorilla costume walk through the screen while the kids toss the ball. They missed something so obvious—a phenomenon psychologists call "intentional blindness." It's a matter of focusing so much of our attention on something that we miss virtually everything around it—even a big, dancing gorilla.

Drew wondered if the same effect might also happen to professionals like radiologists, who are highly trained to identify cancer in lung scans—a skill which is extremely difficult. He gave a group of radiologists a set of scans and asked them to look for cancer nodules. He didn't tell them that he had superimposed an image of a gorilla in the images. Amazingly, 83 percent of the radiologists didn't see the gorilla in the scans.[5] (Can you find it in the image below?)

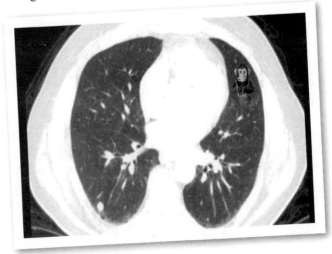

We believe that's what happens day in and day out with most Christians today. We miss God. We're so preoccupied with what we think we're supposed to be doing, we miss the obvious. God is working in our lives all the time, but most of us are too distracted by other things to notice.

We need to be on the look-out for God Sightings. Once you start noticing God in action, you'll see God everywhere. When you do this, you'll find it easy to naturally bring up God in conversations—not as platitudes or quotes—but as real-life examples of God revealing himself to you in your life. God is there, as obvious as daylight, if we only open our eyes.

Fine-tuning your God Sightings lens is a great way to begin sharpening your DIVINE ANTICIPATION skills…and showing God's love to others.

Embody Jesus.

When you practice the 4 ACTS OF LOVE in this book, a transformation will happen because of Jesus working through you. Others will sense your unconditional love for them and your willingness to enter into the mess of real life. They will begin to open up to you because your faith has become more magnetic. In effect, you become their "safe person." You are literally "the body of Christ" (Jesus with skin on) to them.

Your body language speaks volumes when your heart is aligned with God's love, even without saying a word. For example, when someone shares a painful story you can embody empathy by leaning forward, showing concern through your eyes, and keeping your mouth closed more of the time. So often we think we have to *say* something when someone is hurting. Let the peace of Christ dwell in you.

We can't think of a more remarkable example than the one at the beginning of this chapter. Our friend Nathan so humbly and powerfully demonstrates embodying Jesus, even when his life was threatened.

Weave gratitude into every part of your life.

You and the other people in your community probably spend plenty of time being thankful…in November. But outside the Thanksgiving holiday, gratitude gets quickly forgotten. After all, thankfulness is nice, but what does it have to do with a relationship with God?

Here's something to think about: The word "thank" or "thanksgiving" appears more than 100 times in the Bible. God desires our gratitude. Our relationship with God—the very basis of our faith—deepens when we attribute our blessings to God and express our thanks to him.

Research shows that being thankful increases happiness, productivity, self-esteem, spiritual awareness, and good health. Thankfulness makes us less self-centered, worried, envious, physically sick, and materialistic. It brings us closer to God, making us more mindful of his constant presence in our lives.

Gretchen Rubin, author of *The Happiness Project*, told us that thankfulness provides a variety of amazing benefits: "Research shows, and I mean it's just obvious when you think about it, people who have…a mindset of gratitude feel happier. And also gratitude drives out negative feelings like anger or resentment."

One easy way to make this happen is to establish a simple ritual in a regular part of your day. For example, our friend Roma Downey (who starred in the TV show *Touched by an Angel*) starts every day with a small act of thankfulness. "When my first foot hits the floor I say 'thank' and when my second foot hits I say 'you.' Then I say 'thank you' all the way to the bathroom," she said. "A grateful heart is the key to happiness."[6]

Gratitude works for kids as well as adults. Study after study have proven dramatic increases in life satisfaction in a broad array of categories for school children—better grades, better attitudes, less depression, and overall improved happiness.

We believe the more thankful you are, the more you'll be able to love others through DIVINE ANTICIPATION. You'll see God at work more frequently because you're spending more time appreciating his hand in your life. Thankfulness fuels relationships. When it comes to making your faith more magnetic, a grateful person will always be more appealing than someone who takes their life and faith for granted.

> "Therefore, we never stop thanking God that when you received his message from us, you didn't think of our words as mere human ideas. **YOU ACCEPTED WHAT WE SAID AS THE VERY WORD OF GOD—WHICH, OF COURSE, IT IS. AND THIS WORD CONTINUES TO WORK IN YOU WHO BELIEVE.**"
>
> —1 Thessalonians 2:13

Embrace your weakness, so God can be glorified.

Don't view your weaknesses as shortcomings. Look for ways to trust God even more. That surely leads to a complete trust in prayer and God's power, the very definition of DIVINE ANTICIPATION.

As the past few years unfolded, we dove deep into making a documentary film called *When God Left the Building*. Even though we've been creating short-story documentary-style videos for Lifetree Café every week, we've never made a full-length feature documentary film. (Some would say we were crazy!) Yet we felt called to "embrace our weakness," follow God's lead, and talk to people all over the country. We interviewed people from a struggling church in upstate New York; we captured life on the street with a cop, Nathan Matz (the friend we shared about earlier in this chapter); we talked with Rick Warren of Saddleback Church; we listened to others share their stories of joy and pain as we researched the state of the church in America. All to say, we launched into an endeavor that we knew we'd learn from. We know some things, but the project was an example of relying on God in spite of our weaknesses.

We identify with the story of Gideon, who was about to battle thousands of nasty Midianites. (The story can be found in the Bible in the book of Judges, chapter 7.) God knew that if Gideon's army was vast and strong, Gideon may actually think *his own skill and abilities* won the victory. Oh no. God wanted to make sure Gideon's meager army of 300 won the battle, so all glory went to God. "If I let all of you fight the Midianites, the Israelites will boast to me that they saved themselves by their own strength" (Judges 7:2).

We realize so many things happened during the filming that we could only attribute it to God! We think God wanted to remind us it's *his* strength—not ours that miraculously made the film possible. Our team, their skills, the other stories made possible by so many willing to tell their story, being at the right place at the right time…only God could've orchestrated this! To see what we mean, go to WhenGodLeftTheBuilding.com. We had to trust God. We embraced our weakness, so God could be glorified.

Soften your heart.

It's not easy to admit that we might not be as open to loving others—and open to God's action—as we might assume. Most folks (us included!) tend to overestimate just how soft their heart for others really is.

We've taken the *God Space* quiz many times. Honestly, we didn't score very high. But as the years of practicing the 4 ACTS OF LOVE have gone by, we pray God is making us more like him.

Use the *God Space* quiz to reflect on your love for people. Rate yourself and find one or two specific areas in which you can do better.

Reflect on your love for people. Rate yourself.

NEVER				SOMETIMES				ALWAYS	
1	2	3	4	5	6	7	8	9	10

Can you overlook un-Christ-like attitudes and lifestyles in your efforts to connect with others?

1   2   3   4   5   6   7   8   9   10

Are you able to suspend your judgment for long periods of time around not-yet Christians?

1   2   3   4   5   6   7   8   9   10

Do you consistently seek to understand the not-yet Christians you know before seeking to be understood by them?

1   2   3   4   5   6   7   8   9   10

Are you patient enough to wait for the not-yet Christians in your life to ask for your opinion?

1   2   3   4   5   6   7   8   9   10

Be honest: Do you *like* people who are far from God?

1   2   3   4   5   6   7   8   9   10

Do people who are far from God like *you*? For example, are you invited to "party-parties"?

1   2   3   4   5   6   7   8   9   10

Does your body language communicate an open-hearted acceptance of the not-yet Christians in your life?

1   2   3   4   5   6   7   8   9   10

Are you able to communicate acceptance to not-yet Christians without endorsing their lifestyles?

1   2   3   4   5   6   7   8   9   10

In your relationships with not-yet Christians, do you typically offer kindness rather than "rightness"?

1   2   3   4   5   6   7   8   9   10

Is your heart consistently broken and filled with compassion for the not-yet Christians in your life?

1   2   3   4   5   6   7   8   9   10

85 to 100—Congratulations! You might be frequently misunderstood by Christians, but the not-yet Christians in your life are undoubtedly drawn toward the heart of Jesus formed in you. Keep walking in this light.

65 to 85—You must decrease, and Jesus must increase—one heart attitude at a time. Embrace the people and the situations in your life as God attempts to prune those heart attitudes that are not bearing fruit for his kingdom.

Under 65—Jesus needs to do something *in* you before he can do something *through* you. Consider spending less time doing religious activities, and more time asking God to do the soul surgery needed to form the heart of Jesus in you.   Excerpted from *God Space* by Doug Pollock.[7]

Make a beeline to the cross.

You can help others "connect the dots" and make a direct path to Jesus in their daily lives. You can make a connection to Jesus in something as mundane as doing the dishes or as profound as giving birth to a baby. How? Washing dishes can be a picture of Jesus' forgiveness. A newborn can be a sign of new life in Christ. We'll find Jesus wherever we look for him. In every aspect of our lives, Jesus is there.

On the opposite side of that, we need to avoid any actions that point people away from Jesus. As we mentioned earlier, Christians have a terrible reputation for making hideous leaps of judgment, both among those outside the church as well as within. How often do the snide comments, mocking, constant arguing about traditions, and finger pointing turn people away from the Cross of Christ? Please, please, please let our behaviors shine the light of Jesus, not cast dark shadows over his remarkable love.

Be still.

Slow down. Bask in silence. Unplug. We become aware and live DIVINE ANTICIPATION when we pause. Pause. Listen for God. Get quiet. The untethered-from-technology times allow God's still small voice to whisper, "I'm real. I'm here with you. Don't be afraid." Our uber-packed lives rarely allow any margins. But what a wonderful thing—even to pause for a couple minutes. One of our favorite moments of our church's worship service comes when we take a few moments of silence to pray and confess. Ahhhh...breathe...

Of course, we're probably the worst ones to tell others to do this. If you're like us, we cram more things into a day than any sane person should. We don't know why we do that, and we're sure there's some deep psychological reason; nonetheless, we're being honest that when we get still, God surprises us!

Marinate in Scripture.

Read something from the Bible every day. Make reading Scripture a daily habit. It doesn't need to be an obligation. Think of it like showering or brushing your teeth. Simply incorporate a bite-size Bible reading into each day. It's awesome how God's Word is alive and relevant for today. The Holy Spirit seems to revel in giving us an "ah-ha" all the time, no matter how many times we've read through a specific passage. That's what makes the Bible such an extraordinary, miraculous book. The supernatural power of God resides in those pages.

Ever since we've been married, we keep a Bible by the breakfast table. Lately we've been reading a chunk from *The Message*, a down-to-earth paraphrase penned by Eugene Peterson. We love to remind our son, Matt, that when we found out we were pregnant, we were reading the book of Matthew. (Hmmm. Any guesses how our son got his name?)

People who've not recently blown the dust off their family Bible may not know how exhilarating it is to dive into God's Word. There's magnificent, mysterious power in Scripture. To help others get into God's Word, you may want to suggest your friends read the book of John or the four Gospels as a start. The Bible can be intimidating if you're brand-new to its truths. Download the YouVersion of the Bible app. It's free and supplies easy-to-read versions. Dive in!

Here's a brief but important thing to remember as you make the Bible an essential foundation to your life: Spouting Scripture as a way to convince others to believe does not work. Yes, we absolutely believe God's Word has tremendous power. Yet we build barriers to others' growth when we shove it at them. The experience people have with Bible-spraying believers turns them off. Christians must begin really believing that it's God's job to make faith grow. That's what DIVINE ANTICIPATION is all about—letting God do what he does best. Live in the depths of your mysterious, wonderful partnership with Jesus…and relax. Be a friend. Till the soil. And let God do the work beneath the surface.

"God works in different ways, **BUT IT IS THE SAME GOD WHO DOES THE WORK IN ALL OF US.**"

—1 Corinthians 12:6

Welcome others' spiritual experiences.

Because of our weekly conversation café get-togethers, we have the privilege of talking to and listening to people every week. It's not uncommon to hear this phrase: "I've never told anyone this before…." One of the reasons we think others are hesitant to share the depths of their lives (even long-time Christians) is because they think they will be mocked, ignored, preached at, corrected, or condemned. You might be surprised how many

159

people have had inexplicable spiritual encounters that don't fit what we're "supposed" to experience. Let's lift those up rather than discount them.

People everywhere have different or seemingly unusual faith encounters, yet Christians have shut them down because they don't match our predescribed image of what we think God can do. At one Lifetree Café episode on heaven, we sat next to someone who said, "I know. I've died and seen the other side. But I don't tell anybody." As the conversation unfolded, he admitted he'd kept his heavenly experience to himself because he felt others would dismiss him. He described a beautiful experience that he didn't want to leave, but God had more for him to do in this life. Until he felt he had a safe place to share, he kept his God Sighting a secret.

Our friend and co-worker Rodney told us about the time he had what he believes to be an angel encounter. He was hunting with his brother on a snowy day in the Rocky Mountains when they got separated. Rodney got lost. But suddenly, in the most unlikely of spots, there was a man who was inexplicably able to guide him back to his brother, likely saving his life. The only explanation Rodney had for making it out alive is an angelic intervention.

Like Rodney, our God Sightings sometimes may not fit the mold some Christians have set up for themselves. We may find it hard to believe such miraculous encounters occurred in their lives. Yet the more open we are to DIVINE ANTICIPATION, the wider our eyes become and the more freely we'll be able to see God's loving involvement in every corner of our lives.

In light of all that, it's essential that we avoid hanging out only with those who agree with us. We can strengthen our DIVINE ANTICIPATION muscles when we interact with and befriend people who don't see eye to eye with us on every aspect of life. God is working in astonishing ways in lives all around us!

Trust God, realizing you don't know what God is up to.

Release your grip on control, and watch as God orchestrates unexpected results. We have to be completely open to letting the Holy Spirit work. The Spirit reaches each person individually and in a unique and very personal way.

Our friend Sheila told us an extraordinary story about an unexpected encounter she had with a door repairman at the school where she worked. The man had been struggling to get the buzzer operating correctly, so Sheila prayed and ask God to help her make a difference in his life that day. She asked him if his new year had been going well so far. After a pensive pause, the man told her that at Christmas his wife got a call from a 31-year-old woman who said she was the daughter she gave up for adoption 31 years ago. Sheila told us that just the night before she had received her Lifetree Café kit for the week, and the upcoming episode was called "Finding the Family I Never Knew." She told the repairman about it and invited him to attend. He was excited about the possibility of using that event to grow closer to this "new" daughter, as well as show her his Christian side without pushing her away.

Here's another story from our friend Candace. Candace met a young man bagging her groceries at the store. He struck up a conversation and asked what she was doing that weekend. She returned the question. He excitedly told her about his upcoming planned fishing trip with a bunch of buddies.

On her way home she felt compelled, although she wasn't sure why, to pray for him.

The next week at the store, Candace was on her way out. The grocery guy came out of the office door. "Hi! How was your trip?" she asked.

"Fantastic! We had a great time!" he said.

She felt a nudge from God to tell him that she prayed for him. So she told him.

His face immediately went solemn. His eyes raised.

"Thank you. I'm glad you prayed…" Then he gulped. "We were almost killed by a head-on semi!"

A bit stunned, she smiled. God was part of her meeting this young man. You never know what God is up to!

Isn't God amazing? When we expect God to show up, even in the small things—like a broken buzzer or a trip to the grocery store—he doesn't fail to make a loving impact.

Pray, pray, pray.

God wants us to be constantly connected to him, and one of the best ways to remain connected to God is through prayer.

Remember, the 4 ACTS OF LOVE are all about loving others. DIVINE ANTICIPATION comes from knowing that God loves us and wants to make something special happen in our lives. Let's let him. Being in regular communication with him will help us be in tune with God on a regular basis.

One practice we've experienced many times is to pray as if Jesus were sitting in a chair next to you. In his book *Practicing the Presence of Jesus*, pro-golfer Wally Armstrong shares his profound discovery when he began to talk to Jesus (pray) as if he were sitting in a chair next to him.

161

Try it.

Imagine Jesus leaning forward, an eager smile on his face. What might Jesus say to you? What might you and Jesus laugh about? What might you both cry about? What might Jesus ask you? And as he leans in to hug you, what might Jesus whisper in your ear?

Imagine Jesus Saying...

"You're welcome just as you are. Your thoughts are welcome, your doubts are welcome. We're all in this together. And God is here, ready to connect with you in a fresh way."

God is here, ready to connect with you in a fresh way. Are you ready? When you practice love toward others, expecting God to show up, you most certainly are ready.

Endnotes

1. Eugene H. Peterson, *Eat This Book* (Grand Rapids, MI; Eerdmans Publishing, 2006), 160.

2. Ibid.

3. Tamie Harkins, "Making the Church More Accessible to Folks Under 35," *Calling* (blog), April 19, 2011, http://www.fteleaders.org/blog/entry/practical-ideas-making-the-church-more-accessible-to-folks-under-35.

4. Eugene H. Peterson, *Eat This Book* (Grand Rapids, MI; Eerdmans Publishing, 2006), 67.

5. Trafton Drew, "The Invisible Gorilla Strikes Again: Sustained Inattentional Blindness in Expert Observers," Psychological Science, July 17, 2013.

6. Roma Downey, quoted in Kate Meyer, "Notes In My Words—Roma Downey," Ladies' Home Journal, March 2014, 11.

7. Doug Pollock, *God Space* (Loveland, CO: Group Publishing, 2009), 22.

8 LET'S GET STARTED

WE HOPE THIS BOOK HAS INSPIRED YOU to rethink how you live your life as a Christian.

If you care about making your faith magnetic, we know you're the right kind of person who's willing to share God's love through every aspect of your life.

God's love is a truly miraculous gift. We've seen time and time again how the 4 ACTS OF LOVE have helped Christians share that gift with people of all kinds, all stripes, all backgrounds, all beliefs, and all levels of openness. We've watched people's lives transform before our eyes, even those who had completely given up on Jesus and his extraordinary love.

Making your faith magnetic starts with you. Here's what you can do right now:

- Glance back through the book and choose *one* new action. Just one.

- Then practice that one thing. Again and again. Pretend you're learning a new musical instrument or sport.

- Ask trusted friends if they notice any change in you. Welcome their feedback.

- Then pick one new action, and repeat it as often as you can.
- Celebrate what God is doing through you!

We've got a few final notes of encouragement to share before you close this book and continue living your spiritual journey. They're reminders of what it takes to love others through the 4 ACTS OF LOVE: RADICAL HOSPITALITY, FEARLESS CONVERSATION, GENUINE HUMILITY, and DIVINE ANTICIPATION.

> " Remain in me, and I will remain in you. For a branch cannot produce fruit if it is severed from the vine, and **YOU CANNOT BE FRUITFUL UNLESS YOU REMAIN IN ME.** "
>
> —John 15:4

Be a "regular person."

Even God was willing to become a "regular person." God came to us in human form as Jesus. Jesus was God showing us how to be human. Now we, as humans, can show others how to be like God. We are the body of Christ, Jesus "with skin on." What made Jesus/God so astounding while he walked this earth? He interacted with humanity.

Like Jesus, Christians need to get dirty in the mud and muck of people. It's way easier to hide out in the private details of our personal spiritual selves than get messed up in people's lives.

Be a matchmaker.

What if we thought of our role as helping people fall in love with Jesus? Nothing could be more incredible than finding Christ to be the One of your dreams. Falling and staying in love with Jesus promises each person life, hope, passion, commitment, and joy, just like a great marriage. It's powerful. Merely doling out information about God isn't the source of that power. A real relationship with Jesus is.

As a matchmaker it's not our job to *make* someone a Christian. Our role is simply to connect people to Jesus. We set up the date. God's grace lights the fire. And the Holy Spirit takes it from there.

Too often we think the job is up to us. Thankfully, it's not. Isn't that freeing?

Get out of control.

We're not in control, God is.

We don't save people, God does.

Crazy at it seems, God loves us and entrusts his world to us. God is a perfect parent. He's not a dictator parent or a helicopter parent. God sticks with us in the good times and bad, thankfully forgiving us again and again. He loves us and longs to be loved by us.

Fear not!

Fear is your worst enemy.

Our society seems driven by fear. We're afraid of everything, and so we've become more safety-obsessed than ever: seat belts, helmets, knee pads, airport security, metal detectors, safe water, safe air, peanut-free zones, smoke detectors, carbon monoxide detectors, fire alarms, building codes, background checks, warning labels, TV channel blockers, movie and game rating systems, sex offender registries. We don't even allow our kids to play outside anymore for fear of a stranger abducting them.

Christians, too, are engulfed with fear:

- We fear naysayers.
- We fear new and different.
- We fear change.
- We fear doctrinal impurity.
- We fear factual purity.
- We fear deeper relationships with people and instead pursue relationships with ideas.

165

- We fear not knowing all the answers.
- We fear loss of control.
- We fear getting hurt. We don't want to be hurt again.
- We fear that if I accept you, that means I endorse you.
- We fear failure.

No wonder the Bible says "fear not" 366 times—one for every day of the year, plus leap year!

Travel Parable From Antarctica

We see our Antarctica trip as a metaphor for Christians. Others happily listen to our stories and look at our photos so they don't have to go there. We traveled to the tip of South America—"the ends of the earth"—in Ushuaia, Argentina. It was so far from everything that the country originally sent prisoners there to be as far from people as possible.

From this tip of South America we boarded an expedition ship and traveled for two days across the most treacherous seas on the planet. Upon boarding the expedition ship, we noticed sick bags located every 12 inches along the handrails. That was a clue! We tossed and turned through treacherous waves up to 50 feet high. Half the ship's passengers stayed in their staterooms because they were sick. That seafaring trek took us to the continent of Antarctica (which doubles in size in the winter and partially melts away during its summer). It is such a treacherous environment that nothing grows on the rocks. Hardy penguins hoard their pebbles for nests on land, while the sea lions, walruses, and other creatures live underwater. It's here, in this harsh environment, where scientific breakthroughs occur. Scientists and researchers from all countries work together. It's harsh and deadly, yet gloriously beautiful. Icebergs are as magnificent as clouds. God must have such fun creating them both.

The icebreaker ships can poke their way through the ice to open up a passageway, but their captains wisely know enough to realize if it is going to put you in danger. Things might not go the way you planned. You have to trust, live on faith, and accept uncertainty and change. But often it is glorious and worth all the discomfort of getting there.

How is this Antarctica adventure like taking you and your faith to a place it has never gone before?

Some people don't want to go there. And some people are ready for the adventure.

God is with you!

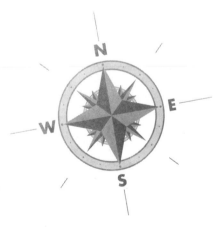

LET'S GET **STARTED**

EPILOGUE

This story is from our friend Mikal, describing our friend Jerry's final days. (Way back in Chapter 1 we mentioned Jerry, the "free thinker" who vocally and candidly questioned Jesus and Christianity.)

One afternoon an email from Jerry landed in my (Mikal's) inbox. He'd been diagnosed with stage 4 prostate cancer, he wrote, and no longer felt up to attending Lifetree. And as his wife, Ruth, was now his full-time caregiver, she'd have to forego attending, too.

We'd interviewed Jerry and Ruth for a Lifetree episode about reincarnation and Jerry and I had shared a number of fairly FEARLESS CONVERSATIONS about that...and God...and politics. Jerry was a lifelong learner, and he leaned into any conversation where he thought he might discover something new.

I wrote back at once. I wondered how staring down the barrel of a terminal prognosis was impacting his beliefs about an afterlife—and if he'd be willing to discuss it.

A typical Jerry response arrived back: He was not only willing, but eager. Trapped in his apartment, Jerry was hungry for good conversation. We scheduled an appointment for the following week between his rounds of doctor visits.

Our Lifetree team wanted to send a card, but what's appropriate for someone in Jerry's situation? Our solution was to gather in front of our Lifetree Café, each of us holding a piece of paper with a word on it. Together, those words sent a message of concern and hope—one Jerry received warmly.

During my first visit, he and Ruth pointed out that our photo was proudly placed on top of a thick stack of cards and notes. It was his favorite.

I saw Jerry a half-dozen times before he went into hospice, and again after he was admitted to that facility. I'd bring along the week's Lifetree program and, as long as he was able to focus through the sharpening pain, we'd talk about the topic...and his failing health.

One afternoon, toward the end, we were frequently interrupted by phone calls. As Ruth fielded yet another one, Jerry groused, "I'm so tired of getting calls from Christians. They know where I stand but don't respect my beliefs. I just want to hang up."

Some of Jerry's Christian callers he knew—and some he didn't. Some expressed a general concern about his spiritual wellbeing but others got right to the point: Unless Jerry made a commitment to Jesus Christ, he'd go to hell. Now was the time to get right with God.

I leaned closer to Jerry and said, "I can tell you why they're calling, if you'd like. What's behind it."

Jerry nodded, and his eyes never left me as I fumbled through an explanation.

"Some of them call and it's really about them. They'll feel guilty if they don't tell you to give your life to Jesus or you're lost. You don't need those people in your life.

"But others are calling because they love you, Jerry. They've found peace and healing in Jesus, and they love you enough to risk your anger to share that with you.

"You need as many of those people in your life as you can get. The trick is knowing which kind of person you've got on the line."

Jerry gave that some thought and then nodded again.

He was drifting, floating off into a haze of pain and medication. It was time for me to go.

Ruth rose to walk me to the door, but I put up a hand to stop her. I could find my own way out. She smiled and said, "When you see your wife, tell her you were out doing good."

I smiled back. "I was out doing 'nice.' If I was doing 'good,' Jerry would have made a personal commitment to Jesus Christ as his Lord and Savior.

Did you do that, Jerry? Have you come to Jesus today?"

Jerry managed a wry grin. "Well, I don't know if I came to Jesus today…
but I do think Jesus came to me."

I walked out the door, found my car, and climbed in.

And cried most of the way home.

A Prayer
FOR YOU FROM US

Love from the center of who you are; don't fake it.

Run for dear life from evil; hold on for dear life to good.

Be good friends who love deeply; practice playing second fiddle.

Don't burn out; keep yourselves fueled and aflame.

Be alert servants of the Master, cheerfully expectant.

Don't quit in hard times; pray all the harder.

Help needy Christians; be inventive in hospitality.

—Romans 12:9-13 *(The Message)*

Let Jesus' love make you irresistible.

4 ACTS OF LOVE JOURNALING

USE THE FOLLOWING PAGES TO REFLECT ON HOW YOU'RE GROWING IN THE

4 ACTS OF LOVE.

JOURNALING:

People I want to show RADICAL HOSPITALITY, and how I plan to do that. (Be sure to come back later and note what happened when you tried those ideas!)

Here's the topic for a FEARLESS CONVERSATION I'd like to try, and the person I'd like to have that conversation with. (What happened? Add that in later.)

JOURNALING:

"Though he was God, he did not think of equality with God as something to cling to. Instead, he gave up his divine privileges; he took the humble position of a slave and was born as a human being. When he appeared in human form, he humbled himself in obedience to God and died a criminal's death on a cross.

"Therefore, God elevated him to the place of highest honor and gave him the name above all names, that at the name of Jesus every knee should bow, in heaven and on earth and under the earth, and every tongue confess that Jesus Christ is Lord, to the glory of God the Father." —Philippians 2:6-11

Let this guide your prayer today as you seek to demonstrate GENUINE HUMILITY.

God is speaking to you. God is moving and at work in your world. But there may be days when, try as you might, it seems you just can't "hear" or "see" God.

Take a moment to think about the circumstances, doubts, stresses, or fears that may prevent you from really seeing God at work in your everyday life. List as many as you can think of here. Then cross them out one by one as you ask God to help you overcome these things and direct you in actions you can take to remove these roadblocks to DIVINE ANTICIPATION.

JOURNALING:

How has God interrupted the busyness of your life in the past few days to draw your focus from the hectic to the eternal? How do you feel God nudging you…pointing you…directing you…pushing you…to *act*?

"We love each other because he loved us first." —1 John 4:19

How was this reflected in your life today?

JOURNALING:

How is God calling you to hit the pavement and put action and effort into the 4 ACTS OF LOVE in your life?

Sketch some walking feet in the space below to show your desire to take action. Near your drawing, write one specific step you'll take this week.

"Most of all, love each other as if your life depended on it. Love makes up for practically anything." —1 Peter 4:8 *(The Message)*

Who in your life needs to receive this kind of love from you this week? What can you do to let this person know you love him or her?

JOURNALING:

What has God shown you this week? What do you suppose he wants you to do about it?

Write it down. Then do it.

"Don't just pretend to love others. Really love them. Hate what is wrong. Hold tightly to what is good. Love each other with genuine affection, and take delight in honoring each other." —Romans 12:9-10

How can you put this into practice today—especially the part about honoring each other?

JOURNALING:

What prayer requests have you brought to God this week with an attitude of DIVINE ANTICIPATION? What else would you like to bring before God?

Write those here.

How does knowing that the all-powerful God loves and pursues you make you feel? How does that knowledge affect your relationship with God?

JOURNALING:

What's the difference between "talking" love and "doing" love? Which are you focusing on most in your life? How can you move from talking to doing?

John 3:16 says that God loved the world so much that he gave his Son. Sometimes it's easier to imagine God loving the world than it is to imagine him loving certain individuals—or even yourself.

Why do you think that is?

JOURNALING:

Take time today to look for connections. An elderly couple taking a stroll together. A mother clutching her child's hand as they cross a street. You exchanging a laugh with a friend.

Jesus wants to be connected to you. He wants a friendship that enables you to live a God-pleasing life.

Capture connections on this page for a few days. Connections between you and others. Between you and God.

"Dear friends, let us continue to love one another, for love comes from God. Anyone who loves is a child of God and knows God. But anyone who does not love does not know God, for God is love." —1 John 4:7-8

Do others experience the love of God by knowing you? How can living out the 4 ACTS OF LOVE be a way of helping them experience God's love through you?

JOURNALING:

"Do not judge others, and you will not be judged. For you will be treated as you treat others." —Matthew 7:1-2

With this in mind, how do you think you will be treated? What judgments are you holding over others that you need to let go of?

When you send a kind card, email, or text, you're letting others know that you're not putting yourself first. You're telling that person, "I've been spending some of my time thinking about you and caring about you."

Choose a person to send a card, email, or text to today. Include a message of love and genuine affirmation.

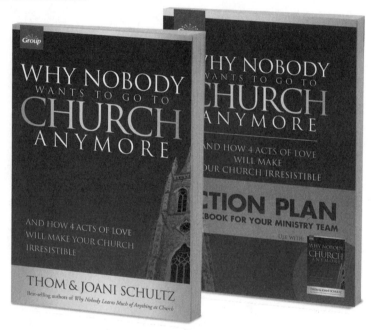